The *Modern* History of Celtic Jewellery
1840-1980

The "Royal Tara Brooch" manufactured by George Waterhouse & Co., Dublin 1850.
Solid, die struck gilt silver, 2.5 inches diameter.

The *Modern* History of Celtic Jewellery
1840-1980

Edited by Stephen Walker

with contributions by Tara Kelly, E. Mairi MacArthur and Aidan Breen

*This book is dedicated to the Celtic artists and craftsmen of old,
the scribes, stone carvers and metalworkers whose legacy
lives on through the continuing tradition they inspired.*

Acknowledgements

Each of the contributing authors has helped tremendously with information, encouragement and connections that go beyond the words that appear in print. Collectors who have kindly lent their treasures are Terry Wheeler, David Martin, Dinah Hoyt Taylor and Gráinne Maguire. Additional photos and illustrations were provided by Groam House Museum and the Iain McCormick Archives, Ola Gorie Jewellery, The National Folklore Collection at University College Dublin, Scottish National Portrait Gallery, and Tadema Gallery, London via the Archibald Knox Society. Alan Cathro or the Iona Shop in Oban and Roy Eprile and staff at Royal Mile Curios in Edinburgh have been helpful by sharing their long experience in the Celtic jewellery business. For proof reading, editing help appreciation is due to Peter Torraca, and Jeanne Walker Todd. The staff at Walker Metalsmiths have all made their contributions to the effort of the exhibit and book , Susanna and Doug Galens, Susette Ordiway, Jessie Grossman, Abram Grossman, Barbara Walker, Lindsey Heavner, and especially Lyndsay Burr who kept the workshop productive while I was otherwise distracted Above all others I am grateful to my wife and business manager Susan Walker. She did most of the photography, patiently helped me through editing and technical problems, but most importantly she helped me find the time and encouraged me to bring this project to completion.

SAW

Published by Walker Metalsmiths
1 Main Street, Andover, New York 14806

ISBN-13: 978-0615805290

ISBN-10: 0615805299

CONTENTS

:

The Authors

Aidan J. Breen. Is a Dublin native trained in his craft by a traditional seven year apprenticeship. "As a young lad, I was always fascinated with the ancient and medieval treasures on display at the National Museum in Kildare Street. This was a place I frequently visited on weekends and still often go for inspiration." Since 1979 he has run his own business, Aidan Breen Gold and Silversmith in Swords, County Dublin.

Dr. E. Mairi MacArthur is from an Iona family and has written extensively about the local history of the island and its people. Her book *Iona Celtic Art. The Work of Alexander and Euphemia Ritchie*, published by The New Iona Press, is a very thorough history of Iona jewellery. She is a graduate of St Andrews University and later undertook her doctoral research into Iona at the School of Scottish Studies, University of Edinburgh.

Dr. Tara Kelly is an independent art historian and curator. Her dissertation at Trinity College, Dublin focused on copies of Irish archaeological jewellery and metalwork made in Dublin between 1840 and 1940. Her research into the production methods, marketing strategies and distribution of copies of Irish antiquities represents a significant advancement in our knowledge of this industry.

Stephen Walker is a goldsmith specializing in Celtic design. He is a graduate of Syracuse University earning his Masters of Fine Arts at Southern Illinois University at Carbondale. With his wife Susan they run Walker Metalsmiths, established 1984 in Andover, New York.

Introduction

The jewelry illustrated in this volume formed the body of an exhibition displayed at Walker Metalsmiths in Fairport, NY during the spring of 2013 and again in Andover, NY in March 2016. The term "Modern" in the title of the book and exhibition is used in the sense of the period since the Industrial Revolution. The concept of this project has had a tendency to be confusing to the audience since it is neither a review of Celtic jewelry of the present, nor a history of ancient or medieval Celtic jewelry. It is a history of Celtic jewelry from the beginning of the Celtic Revival, which began in the 1840s, up to the beginnings of the present Celtic Renaissance, which was taking shape in the 1980s.

The desire to revive and savor the splendid cultural heritage of the past is very similar today as it was 150 years ago. The Celtic Renaissance is as much an echo of the Celtic Revival as it is inspired by the early medieval Golden Age of Celtic Art. The tendency of always viewing modern Celtic jewelry as something medieval was shaped by the way Celtic Revival expressions of the symbolic and ornamental tradition was made and presented in the past two centuries. At first direct copies were made as precisely as possible. Gradually adaptations and innovations began to creep in. Even when the modern designer creates something new and original, if that creation is done in the traditional style, our cultural inclination treats it as if it is already old, and that its authenticity must flow from a prototype in the past. Despite the fact that the truly fluent use of Celtic design and ornament is creative and original, the habit of viewing it all as something ancient is a strong one. The jewelry designers of today's Celtic Renaissance are following a tradition that has evolved. We hope that the pages that follow succeed somewhat in shedding light on this material as the product of the more recent past.

The collection accumulated by the Walker family has been supplemented with loans from Terry Wheeler, David Martin, Dinah Hoyt Taylor and Gráinne Maguire. There are some things that are absent, not due to a lack of trying to arrange loans, but because they are rare, valuable and difficult to locate. The jewelry of Manx designer Archibald Knox, which was manufactured by Liberty & Co. from 1899 to 1917, was extremely influential in the modern evolution of Celtic jewelry. Since the story of the Celtic Revival and the use of Celtic ornament in the applied arts cannot be accurately told without a reference to Knox, we include a photo provided by the Archibald Knox Society, although no actual example was available for the exhibit. There are certainly other craftsmen, companies and trends that deserve a place in this history.

An explanation is in order regarding the spelling and measurement systems used in these pages. Units of measure are part of a culture. Dimensions of the pieces illustrated are given in inches rather than the more common contemporary convention of using metric measurements. If a brooch is 51 millimeters in diameter, it is because the craftsman was using Imperial measure and laid it out as two inches. British spelling is used by the contributing authors from Scotland and Ireland, but Stephen Walker's essay is presented in American spelling.

The Time Machine

Stephen Walker

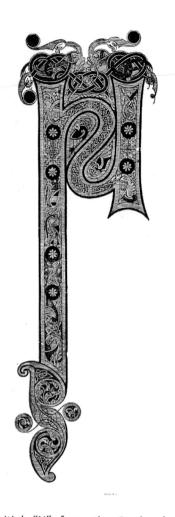

*Initial "N" from the **Book of Kells**. This woodcut detail of the 8th century illuminated manuscript is from* Early Christian Art in Ireland *by Margaret Stokes, 1887. Beginning in the 19th century most people became aware of Celtic art, not from actual exposure to the medieval sources, but by viewing reproductions and illustrations. Taking a detail like this off the original page caused the viewer to see it differently than if it was in the context of the whole book. This also led to the creative re-use of these details as stand-alone designs.*

The ancient traditions of Celtic jewelry have become a part of how the Irish, Scots, Welsh and other nationalities of Celtic heritage expressed their cultural identity. The story usually told of this tradition focuses on very old prototypes, the museum pieces turned up by archaeologists or the legend of the original Claddagh ring. In our minds, we connect the popular Celtic jewelry of today with the distant past. This exhibit and commentary tells the story of the more recent past, from the beginnings of the Celtic Revival in the 1840s to a resurgence of interest in the 1980s, which has come to be called the Celtic Renaissance. We tend to imagine our heritage on a grand time scale of centuries and millennia. The Celtic jewelry of today reaches back to the great medieval masterpieces of Celtic art, but that link with the ancient style is very much influenced by what others had done in more recent history. What we get from the generations of our parents and grandparents is our bridge to the past and certainly a valuable and authentic inheritance.

Medieval masterpieces such as the *Book of Kells*, the Tara Brooch and the Ardagh Chalice are brought to mind when we see the intricate knots, spirals and interlaced beasts that have become the emblematic style of Celtic heritage. The symbols and motifs of the Celtic Golden Age of 650 to 900 A. D. have traveled from long ago to our own time as an expression of tradition and pride of ancestry. The artifacts of that bygone era are evidence that our Dark Age ancestors were not simply backward barbarians beyond the edge of civilization. They were capable of great sophistication and beautiful cultural accomplishments.

My pedigree for Celtic art was limited. As a school boy I became interested in Celtic art after my grandmother visited Ireland in 1968. She brought me back a little souvenir book about the *Book of Kells*. My teen years were centered on playing bagpipes in a band of Americans of Scottish and Irish ancestry. Among bagpipe students it was a regular topic of conversation; who you learned from and who their tutors were. At a summer session of the Invermark College of Piping in Petersburgh, NY a chart was shown that traced the succession of our teachers back through the ages to the MacCrimmons on the Isle of Skye in the 16th century. As I tried my hand at making pipe band regalia, I developed a love of metalwork that became my career.

Like most craftsmen working with Celtic designs I looked to the distant past for inspiration and offered it as a reference of what my own work was all about. Yet modern Celtic artists claim to be part of a living artistic tradition. If these claims are valid, then there must be more recent generations of this heritage.

My art teacher, William "Scotty" MacCrea taught Celtic art. Though he was encouraged by his older family members in his own youth, he gained his knowledge and skill mainly through observation and his own talent and study. His passion for Celtic art and tradition fueled much of my early interest in Celtic art, history, and bagpiping. In 1975, after High School, I spent a year traveling in the British Isles. There I saw some modern Celtic art in the restoration of the Abby on Iona and a smattering of Celtic jewelry, sold mostly in tourist shops. A bright spot was the Iona Shop in Oban that sold the Celtic jewelry of John Hart. For the most part Celtic art was very elusive as a living tradition. What little Celtic jewelry I did encounter was presented as if it came to the present through a time machine, which in a way it had, since you can learn at least something from the study of older artwork through observation and imitation.

In 1977 The Treasures of Early Irish Art exhibit toured the United States bringing the *Book of Kells* and most of the other major medieval treasures from the National Museum of Ireland to several major American art museums. I saw this exhibit at the Metropolitan Museum of Art in New York. The publicity surrounding this cultural exchange created a great deal of awareness, as did the Work of Angels exhibit in 1989-1990. The Work of Angels exhibit collected together many of the greatest masterpieces of Celtic metalwork from the collections of the National Museums of Ireland and Scotland as well as the British Museum. That exhibit, which toured all three museums, included the Tara Brooch, the Ardagh Chalice, the St. Ninian's Isle Treasure and many more splendid pieces from the 6th – 9th centuries AD. The publications that accompanied both of these exhibits and the strong media coverage were an inspiration to a whole new generation of craftsmen. It also energized a new audience whose appetites and imaginations had been excited by the treasures they had seen. The craftsmen that had already been producing Celtic style

The Ardagh Chalice. This 8th century silver, gold and bronze masterpiece of Celtic metalwork was discovered by some boys digging potatoes in 1868. It has become as iconic an image of Ireland as the Book of Kells or the Tara Brooch.

Jacobite dirk made from a cut-down sword blade, bog oak handle with copper hilt and top plate. 18th century, 14 inches long. The crude interlace design of this dirk betrays that the craftsman was not fluent in the conventions of Celtic design, yet the fact that it was important enough to try to copy the archaic style shows how it had become significant for a Highlander to be outfitted with images of a distinct cultural past.

jewelry, such as Ola Gorie, Aidan Breen, and established companies like Celtic Art Ltd. and Hebridean Jewellery were in a perfect position to ride the wave of enthusiasm and increased sales from this trend. Many start-ups joined into what has come to be known as the Celtic Renaissance.

The Celtic Renaissance is really the second wind of the 19th century Celtic Revival. In fact Celtic art has undergone a number of revivals since its Golden Age. In the 12th century what was already an archaic style was resurrected as a self-conscious reference to the past. Thus monuments, reliquaries and instruments of office, such as high crosses and bishops' crosiers, could be made as a form of visual propaganda. Upstart dynasties mimicked the trapping of their well established rivals. This happened again during the Gaelic Renaissance in the West Highlands and Hebrides as the Lords of the Isles flaunted their independence and unique cultural heritage in the 14th and 15th centuries. During the 17th and 18th centuries, interlaced designs were again deployed as part of the regalia of the Jacobite uprisings in Scotland. The designs were used to decorate the weapons of rebellion and the brooches worn by kilted Highland clansmen.

These older revivals are all sufficiently medieval and beyond living memory that we can think of them as one long continuum of tradition. The modern era, since the Industrial Revolution, the advent of archaeology, mass communications, advertising and middle class tourism presents Celtic art to our generation in a similar way that previous revivals did. The old style was imitated and it is used to claim a connection to the glories of a proud heroic past.

But how did this transition into the Celtic jewelry of today? As my own jewelry business grew my customers expected me to be an expert, not only as a craftsman but as an historian. The increasingly common *from-the-Book-of-Kells* answer seemed somewhat shallow, since it ignored more than a thousand years between then and now. In the early 1990s I began looking for other craftsmen who could supply jewelry to give my customers greater depth of selection. The mark "Iona" kept coming up on Scottish Celtic jewelry I encountered in the US. I made an inquiry to the Iona Shop in Oban and was informed that there was no such company as "Iona Silver" or "Iona Jewelry" and that their wares were purchased from a number of different producers. I then began making annual trips to trade fairs in Scotland and Ireland. The craftsmen I met as suppliers for my business often became friends, as well as informants in my search for answers about how modern Celtic jewelry had evolved. Some jewelers in Scotland had roots in the "Iona" tradition. Most were inspired and influenced by the Work of Angels exhibit and by the book *Celtic Art; the Methods of Construction* by Scottish art teacher George Bain (1881-1968). Visiting Scotland in 1995 I discovered an exhibit at the Iona Heritage Centre about the silver jewelry and brassware of Alexander Ritchie. Ritchie, with his wife Euphemia Thomson, had run a business called Iona Celtic Art from 1899 until their deaths in 1941. A small book of designs and some commentary by Iain McCormick accompanied the exhibit. McCormick had been an apprentice to the Ritchies in his youth and followed a career as a jewelry artisan and art teacher. Eventually I made contact with historian E. Mairi MacArthur, whose works includes the book *Iona Celtic Art; the Work of Alexander and Euphemia Ritchie*. Dr. MacArthur's contribution to this volume begins on page 37.

Silver cross manufactured by Hamish Dawson-Bowman from an earlier Alexander Ritchie pattern. 2.5 x 1 inch. Late 1940s.

"Iona" had become something of a brand name for Scottish Celtic jewelry due to the efforts of the Ritchies. After World War II a number of craftsmen and businesses used the "Iona" mark, beginning with Iain McCormick and his mother Hanna. They had inherited the Ritchie patterns and stock. For a time they sold Ritchie designs under a cottage industry shop on the island called Highland Home Industries. Industrialist Hamish Dawson-Bowman set up a company called Celtic Art Industries. Dawson-Bowman hired Iain McCormick as well as craftsmen John Hart and Malachi Gormly to provide training and work for disabled veterans of the war as well as to continue the tradition of Iona Celtic Art. McCormick and Hart left the company after several years, each to pursue their art in different ways. Dawson-Bowman set up a second company in 1968, Art Pewter, which continues to make plated pewter Celtic jewelry and other Scottish themed accessories under the management of Hamish Dawson-Bowman's grandsons, David, Stephen and Mark. The silver and gold side of the company became Celtic Art Ltd after it was passed to silversmith Andy Hynd upon Hamish Dawson-Bowman's death in 1974. John Hart and Iain McCormick both continued to produce Celtic jewelry under their own marks and both continued to use the "Iona" mark as well.

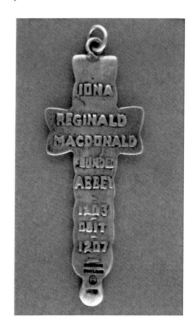

Like any family tree, modern Celtic jewelry has more than one branch. On the Irish side, Dr. Tara Kelly tells, in her following essay, how the commercial craftsmen of the Celtic Revival in Dublin produced facsimiles of early Irish brooches and other metalwork.

Brooch of silver, red jasper, bloodstone and granite. 1.75 inch. Unmarked, Scottish, circa 1870-1900.

Beginning in the 1840s some of the most up-to-date technology was used to manufacture these objects. The marketing used the emerging mass communications of advertising and promotion at world's fairs. The message of the Celtic Revival was to channel pride in artistic accomplishments of the past into the present. The copies were adapted in size and fitted with modern pin catches to make them somewhat more wearable. They appealed to national vanity and an idealized past.

In Victorian Scotland "Scotch pebble" jewelry was mass produced using stamping dies and specialized trades for cutting and polishing stones. Sometimes these pieces were designed to follow the form of traditional Celtic pieces, but only rarely did they feature any Celtic ornament like we see on the cross on page __. It may come as a surprise that in both Scotland and Ireland, the earliest Victorian jewelry that was presented as a stereotypically national style was not the folk art product of cottage industries. In fact it was manufactured using the latest Industrial Revolution techniques, specialized skilled labor and presented to the public through slick marketing and advertising. The trend towards a more handmade look in Celtic jewelry does not begin until the end of the century.

In 1899 Alexander and Euphemia Ritchie began their business on Iona and Archibald Knox (1864-1933) began work for Liberty and Co. Both were very influenced by the Arts and Crafts Movement. Knox was the main designer for the 'Cymric' and 'Tudric' Celtic range of handmade metalwork, frequently described as British Art Nouveau. This was manufactured and sold by the London department store Liberty and Co. Rather than basing his designs on specific historical models Knox worked in an abstract style that captures the spirit of interlace design. In his jewelry Knox liberates the knot from its background and uses it to form the entire structure of his jewelry pieces. Knox's designs are not copied from historical sources, but are original modern creations. Ritchie also created original modern designs, but continued to do a great deal of work that is directly copied from historical sources or is adapted from them.

Gold and enamel necklace designed by Archibald Knox for Liberty & Co. Knox's breakaway designs for Liberty were done between 1899 and 1917, however he was not publicly acknowledged as the designer at the time. Photo by Tadema Gallery, London.

The Arts and Crafts Movement in Ireland embraced the Celtic style early on, but began to back away in the 1920s. The governor of the National Gallery of Ireland, Thomas Bodkin, writing in *The Studio* magazine in 1921, drew attention to the decline in Celtic ornament in the Sixth Exhibition of the Arts and Crafts Society of Ireland said, "National art all over the world has burst long ago, the narrow boundaries within which it is cradled, and grows more cosmopolitan in spirit with each succeeding generation." George Atkinson, writing the foreword to the catalogue of that same exhibit emphasized the society's disapproval of any undue emphasis on Celtic ornament at the expense of good design. "Special pleading on behalf of the national traditional ornament is no longer justifiable."[*] The style had served the nationalist cause as an emblem of a distinct Irish culture, but soon intellectual fashions abandoned Celtic art as nostalgically looking backwards. The elites of a newly independent Ireland sought to involve themselves in the revolutionary modernist ideas of the 20th century. On the isolated Isle of Iona the Ritchies continued their enterprise for their own reasons, while the Celtic style faded from fashion in jewelry in Ireland.

Celtic ornament continued to be used in Ireland for other purposes that were by nature patriotic, such as monuments and the decoration for official state documents. Gaelic Athletic Association emblems and prizes, currency design and costumes for Irish dance have been dominated by Celtic art since independence. Celtic styled souvenirs for the tourist trade also continued to be supplied in the form of jewelry, but the Celtic theme in mainstream fashion faded from jewelry in Ireland after the 1920s. Silversmiths did, however, continue to produce Celtic designs for ecclesiastical vessels and church furnishings as well as silverware for domestic use.

Aidan Breen, when he began his apprenticeship in 1959 in the Dublin silver trade, was so surrounded with what remained of a shrinking tradition that he barely noticed that Celtic art was a dying art during his early career. Later on, as a talented and still young craftsman he was in a unique position when public interest in Celtic design was reborn in the 1980s. The silver industry in Ireland preserved the Celtic art tradition of the 19th and early 20th centuries so that while most craftsmen and designers of the Celtic Renaissance were starting from scratch, Aidan Breen was a living link to the old Celtic Revival, thoroughly trained in old-school craftsmanship, reinforced by his personal love and study of the original source material.

In the 1980s Celtic jewelry was making a comeback in popularity. By the 1990s the number of new craftsmen, designers and retailers

The term "Tara Brooch" became generic for any brooch of a similar shape. This unmarked silver and enamel pin was a uniform accessory of Cumann na mBan, an Irishwomen's paramilitary organization that was an auxiliary of the Irish Volunteers. 1.5 x 1.25 inch, Second quarter 20th century.

---

[*] Paul Larmour, *The Arts and Crafts Movement in Ireland*, Friar's Bush Press, Belfast 1992, pg 201

specializing in Celtic jewelry was rapidly increasing. The people involved ranged from hippies to mainstream jewelry manufacturers and entrepreneurs who outsourced their production. For a while the increase in demand was a bonanza for many of the older producers who already had full ranges of designs. A respectable number of new independent craftsmen joined the field. Some new comers were art school graduates; others had previous careers in business and industry.

The Celtic Renaissance has been an international phenomenon, with participants no longer confined to just the Old-World Celtic countries. Certainly there are a number of interesting enterprises that started since 1980. But, for now we will content ourselves to look at the history of how the Celtic Revival emerged from the nearly burned out embers of an ancient art and established a modern tradition. That tradition still involves imagining the distant past, but the purpose of this project is to remember the recent history of this art, for memory is the time machine that delivered this heritage to our generation.

SAW

Dunvegan Teapot, Sterling silver marked "West & Son" with assay stamps for Dublin 1914. 9.5 x 6.5 x 5.5 inches.
West did not manufacture themselves and this piece was created by Wakley & Wheeler, *the firm that later became Alwright and Marshalls and was still producing this design in the 1970s.*

Previous page: Angus Mackay, 1812 - 1859. Piper to Queen Victoria, 1843 – 1853 *by Alexander Johnson 1840. The fully accessorized kilted Highlander with jeweled dirk, brooches, buckles. The small knife worn in the stocking is a sgian dubh, Gaelic for "black knife", that follows the design conventions of the dirk on a smaller scale. Scottish National Portrait Gallery.*

A Scottish dirk is a dagger that was a fighting weapon of the Jacobite period. In the later 18th century and down to the present, a dirk is an accessory to be worn by a man with a kilt, more as an emblem of tradition than as a practical tool. The characteristic style of a Scottish dirk has a thistle shaped wooden handle carved with an interlaced design. By the early 19th century this Celtic style had all but disappeared from the fashions for other decorative objects but interlace knotwork persisted on the handles of dirks. Tradition minded Highlanders preserved this motif as a still burning ember of the medieval legacy of Celtic ornament.

Left: A child's dirk, carved wooden handles, white metal and faux Cairngorm gems. 10 inches long.

Center: Jeweled dirk, unmarked silver mounts and glass gems, equipped with smaller knife and fork for dining.18 inches long. Circa 1900-1910. In Victorian times the fashion for decorating dirks with Cairngorm jewels, amber colored quartz stones, native to the Scottish Highlands, as well as employing thistle designs in the ornament further emphasize the purpose of the dirk as an icon of Scottishness.

Right: Sgian Dubh. Sterling silver, wood, faux cairngorm. 8 inches long. Edinburgh hallmarks for 1957

"**Scotch Pebble**" or agate jewellery gained fashionable acceptance in Scotland as a direct result of the young Queen Victoria and Prince Albert having pebbles that they had personally found on the Queen's Balmoral Estate made into gifts for each other and for their friends and family. As middle class tourism became much more common in the late 19th century, the fashion for jewellery as souvenirs accelerated the growth of this colourful style. Local materials, such as the Montrose agates, Aberdeen granites and Cairngorm citrines were combined with distinctly Scottish styles and motifs. Kilt pins were often made in the form of bladed weapons associated with the romantic image of the kilted clansman. Beginning around 1850 manufacturers, first in Aberdeen and then in Edinburgh, manufactured an imaginative variety of colorful jewelry, eventually contracting the production out to Birmingham and even Germany. Typically the metal portion of the jewellery is soldered together from stamped silver shells, produced by steel dies. The stones are then cemented in place, often filing the hollow silver or gold body of the piece with a mixture of shellac. Usually hand engraved scrolls, wiggles, and bright cuts finish the designs. These pieces were mass produced using expensive tooling, dies and stamping presses, but also requiring highly skilled jewelers for the soldering, engraving, and the skilled lapidary work to cut, polish, and fit the stones. The manufacture of pebble jewellery flourished from the 1860s to the First World War. Some production continues to the present and the style is frequently imitated since the 1960s using cast base metal settings. In the popular Harry Potter movies (1997 -2011) the character Professor McGonnagall, played by Margaret Smith, speaks with a Scottish accent and her costume is accessorized with a distinctive pebble brooch that further establishes her Scottish identity.

Opposite page:

A. *Primitive silver Luckenbooth brooch with buckle style pin. 1.25 x 1 inch. Engraved on the back with the initials "FF". No other marks. 18th century.*
B. *Victorian Luckenbooth brooch with clan crest. Silver, partial gilt. 2.5 x 2.25 inch. No marks.*
C. *Luckenbooth set with citrine gem stone. Marked "IONA" "JH" and Edinburgh hallmarks for 1973-74. This was a premium hand cut and hand engraved piece made by* John Hart *exclusively for the Iona Shop and marketed as the "Holyrood Luckenbooth Brooch".*
D. *Hand engraved Luckenbooth on a die-cut silver blank. 1.9 x 1.5 inch. Ward Brothers. Hallmarks: WBs, Edinburgh 1967-68*
E. *Cast silver Luckenbooth John Hart, 1.75 x 1.25 inch. Marked: "IONA", "JH", "SCOTLAND" & "SILVER". No assay marks.*

This Celtic cross is unusual for pebble jewellery in that it is decorated with an interlace design. Silver, jasper, bloodstone and glass. 2 x 1.6 inch.
Scottish circa 1880.

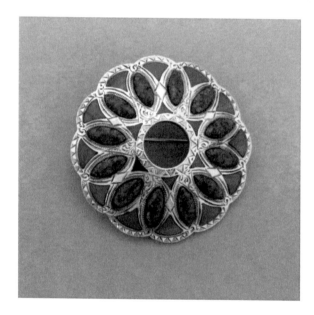

Agate and Aberdeen granite pebble brooch.
2.25 inch diameter. Circa 1870.

Left: Bog oak and green marble Celtic Cross pendants.1.25 x .75 inch. The materials are in themselves symbolic as both are materials that came to be emblematically associated with nation and heritage. Irish bog oak was used for a number of decorative purposes, as was Iona marble and Connemara marble.

The Luckenbooth brooch gains it name from the "locked booths" that sold trifles along the Royal Mile near Saint Giles Cathedral in High Street Edinburgh. In its simplest form it is a single heart shape with an open center that works with a buckle pin like an annular brooch. The heart and crown motifs are part of the same 17th century fashion trends that resulted in the Claddagh ring design in Ireland. Two hearts intertwined; with and without crowns, as well as various abstractions and embellishments give this quite simple type of brooch many delightful forms. Quite commonly given as a love token or betrothal gift, folklore also invests the Luckenbooth brooch with talismanic value for protection against evil-eye and for nursing mothers to avoid witches stealing their milk or harming their babies. Legend associates the Luckenbooth brooch with Mary Queen of Scots (1542-1587). The form with two hearts and crown can be read as a romantic abstraction of the letter "M" in a royal monogram. Surprisingly silver Luckenbooth brooches were a popular trade item with American Indians in the 18th century, especially the Iroquois Nations. The design remains a traditional jewelry accessory and is even called "Luckenbooth" by contemporary Native-Americans.

The Luckenbooth brooch has been a self-consciously Scottish form of jewellery since the 19th century. The form was adapted to pebble jewellery in Victorian times, as well as being a regular feature in the ranges of most Scottish manufacturing jewellers who worked for the Highland outfitter and tourist trades.

Cavan Brooch, Inscription on the back in raised letters that are moulded right into the tooling: "West & Company Registered 1849" Hollow gilt silver 2.25 inches diameter. A facsimile of this pattern executed in Wicklow gold with a large Irish river pearl was created as a gift from the Provost and Senior Fellows of Trinity College to Queen Victoria to mark the occasion of her visit to the Library Subsequently this brooch was also known as the "Queen's Brooch". Commissioned by West & Co and manufactured by Edmond Johnson Jr. See pages 26 & 27.

Londesborough Brooch.
No marks. Hollow silver,
2 inch diameter

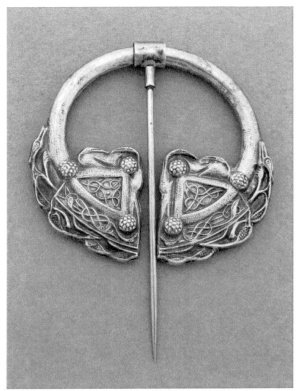

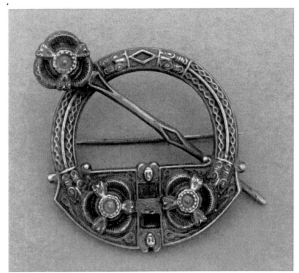

Cavan Brooch, Marked: "A&LLd" for Adie & Lovekin Ltd. *Birmingham hallmarks for 1912-13. Silver, hollow, 1.5 inch diameter.*

Loughan Brooch. No marks, hollow silver, 2 inch diameter hoop.

The piece above functions as a true penannular brooch with a swiveling pin that can slide along the hoop between the triangular terminals. The other brooches illustrated on this and the facing pages have fixed non-functional pins representative of the design of the original medieval artifacts. Smaller pins with catches on the back that are designed for wear with contemporary clothing are typical of Celtic Revival facsimile brooches, however a certain number do function in the manner of the originals.

Kilmainham Brooch, marked: B.W.E. Pantentee, 2 inch diameter

Fig. 1　　　　*Clarendon Brooh*

Amongst the Rare and Beautiful Collection of Antiquities at the Royal Irish Academy are some choice Specimens of Brooches, which were worn by the Irish Chieftains about the Tenth Century. WATERHOUSE and COMPANY, anticipating that the revival of those Brooches of the "olden time" would find favour in the present day, have by registration secured the pattern of two of them, and have already manufactured a great number for the Nobility and Gentry. As Shawl or Cloak Fasteners they are perfectly safe, and in this respect can stand the test with, if not surpass, any modern invention. The stems are not stationary or secured at the point by the ordinary catch, but revolve similarly to a key on a ring, and, passing through a space left for their admission, are afterwards moved round to another position, and rest upon the strongest portion of the Brooch, from which the most violent exercise could not disturb them. WATERHOUSE and COMPANY with pride and pleasure announce that Her Excellency the Countess of Clarendon having been pleased to testify her approval of one of these Specimens of Modern Antique, they have ventured to grace it by the designation of THE CLARENDON SHAWL BROOCH.

Waterhouse & Company Advertisement
Freeman's Journal and Daily Commercial Advertiser
11 March 1850

"Specimens of Modern Antique":
Commercial Facsimiles of Irish Archaeological Jewellery, 1840-1868

Tara Kelly

By the middle of the nineteenth century Ireland was increasingly defined by a national identity rooted in the Celtic past, in which artefacts, architectural monuments and historic sites played a central role.[1] Facsimiles (or copies) of Irish archaeological jewellery appeared in Ireland as a new type of commercial merchandise that served as a material link between the past and the present, a representation of the continuity of a distinctively Irish tradition of design and craftsmanship from the earliest periods of Irish history through the modern age. As products of the Celtic Revival, facsimiles were an expression of the growing popular interest in Irish antiquities, paralleled by a renewed study of Irish music, literature, theatre, dancing and sport. The inspiration to copy Irish artefacts also appears to have been a response to the wider European trend for archaeological-style jewellery that had developed by the 1840s, including the reproduction of Etruscan and Greek jewellery by the Castellani firm in Rome, as well as designs based on Gothic and Renaissance jewellery by the firm of Froment-Meurice in Paris and by A.W.N. Pugin in London.[2] The emergence of modern shopping culture across Europe, resulting from advances in manufacturing technologies and mass-production, widespread media consumption and advertising, and the establishment of large-scale marketplaces such as department stores and industrial exhibitions, helped fuel demand for Irish heritage jewellery from individual customers at home and overseas. The broad educational mission of museums during this period created an environment in which facsimiles of Irish archaeological jewellery were acquired both as outstanding examples of modern industrial design

around the world. Facsimiles of Irish archaeological jewellery enabled works of surpassing beauty and fundamental importance to become more widely accessible and reinforced the status of the original artefacts as national symbols used to express concepts of 'Irishness' that persist today.

The major retailers and manufacturers engaged in the Irish facsimile industry were Waterhouse & Company, West & Son, William Acheson, Joseph Johnson Jr., Edmond Johnson Jr. and Hopkins & Hopkins. In 1842 George Waterhouse of Sheffield, England opened a Dublin branch of his firm, Waterhouse & Company, at 25 Dame Street under the management of his son, Samuel S. Waterhouse.[3] West & Son, a firm established by a prominent Dublin family of goldsmiths, silversmiths and jewellers active in the trade since the eighteenth century, was located at 18-19 College Green from 1846.[4] William Acheson, in partnership with another local craftsman, Barnett Boam, established his firm in 1850 at 109 Grafton Street.[5] Brothers Joseph Johnson Jr. and Edmond Johnson Jr. were members of another well-known family of Dublin goldsmiths, silversmiths and jewellers dating back to the eighteenth century, who began their careers working in branches of the family firm.[6] Both later went on to operate as independent manufacturers and retailers, with Joseph Johnson Jr. based at 22 Suffolk Street from c. 1860 and Edmond Johnson Jr. located at 89 Grafton Street by 1867.[7] The firm of Hopkins & Hopkins was established in 1868 at 1 Lower Sackville Street, later renamed O'Connell Street.[8] Although the production of facsimiles of Irish archaeological jewellery was initially a sideline, these

Fibula Brooch.
Fig 2

six Dublin retailers and manufacturers went on to make it a central feature of their business in response to successful publicity and sales, resulting in the emergence of the Celtic Revival jewellery industry in Ireland.

Irish facsimile production formally began in 1842 with the 'Fibula' brooch (Fig. 2), a composite design based on Late Bronze Age gold ornaments and sold by Waterhouse & Company as modern pieces of jewellery.[9] The 'Fibula' brooch was created by copying elements from gold dress-fasteners and ear-ornaments dating from c. 900-700 BC in the Royal Irish Academy collection, which were then combined and adapted to form a new design for a brooch available in multiple sizes, metals and finishes.[10] Official credit for the suggestion to copy and rework the originals was given to Corry Connellan, then private secretary to

the Earl of Clarendon, Lord Lieutenant of Ireland, which seems designed to encourage future patronage from Dublin Castle and the Anglo-Irish ascendancy.[11] As one of the earliest documented facsimiles of Irish archaeological-style jewellery, the 'Fibula' brooch may have been introduced by Waterhouse & Company to coincide with the opening of their Dublin branch, creating a particularly 'Irish' type of jewellery designed to appeal to fashionable customers with an interest in Irish history, traditions and artefacts.

The production of facsimiles of Irish archaeological jewellery received a significant boost in 1849 from two key events: the Royal Irish Academy museum opened its doors to members of the general public, granting more people access to their extensive collection of Irish artefacts, and an official royal visit to Ireland by Queen Victoria and Prince Albert took place.[12] Public and privately held collections of Irish jewellery and metalwork served as historical design sources and the starting point for facsimiles, with Dublin unquestionably at the centre of facsimile production due to the presence of numerous major collections that were the focus of art historical and archaeological scholarship. The Royal Dublin Society, Trinity College Library and the Royal Irish Academy held the most important collections of Irish material culture, which were repeatedly drawn upon by retailers and manufacturers for artistic inspiration. The increased public access to original artefacts in the Royal Irish Academy, granted within the first six months of 1849, resulted in an explosion of new designs for facsimiles of Irish archaeological jewellery, mainly brooches. The scheduled royal visit to Dublin in August 1849 spurred local retailers and manufacturers to produce merchandise that would be understood as intrinsically 'Irish' to encourage patronage from the royal family and the upper echelons of British and Irish society. The potential impact of such patronage had already been demonstrated in Scotland after the royal acquisition of Balmoral Castle in 1848 and the resultant promotion of Highland dress and associated types of 'national' jewellery, particularly 'pebble jewellery' made with local Scottish stones, by the royal family.[13] Presumably the Dublin firms wanted to capitalise on the commercial opportunity presented by the royal visit to create Irish merchandise that would have a similar appeal.

In 1849 Waterhouse & Company issued the 'Clarendon' brooch (Fig. 1), named for the Countess of Clarendon, wife of the Lord Lieutenant of Ireland.[14] The design for the 'Clarendon' brooch was an amalgamation of two Hiberno-Viking brooches discovered in the early nineteenth century. The main body of the 'Clarendon' brooch was a reduced-size copy of a large tenth-century brooch from Virginia, Co. Cavan owned by the Royal Irish Academy.[15] An inscription in *Ogham*, an ancient form of Irish writing, was copied from the back of a tenth-century brooch from Ballyspellan, Co. Kilkenny in the Royal Dublin Society and reproduced on the back of the 'Clarendon' brooch.[16] Under copyright legislation enacted in 1842, the 'Clarendon' brooch was registered for a three-year period of commercial protection to ensure exclusivity.[17] It was, however, Joseph Johnson Jr. who registered the design for the 'Clarendon' brooch on 25 July 1849, which may be explained by his possible role as manufacturer for Waterhouse & Company during this period.[18]

The Ballyspellan brooch was the first example of archaeological jewellery found in Ireland with an *Ogham* inscription, a feature exploited by Waterhouse & Company in their stock catalogues to market the 'Clarendon' brooch.[19] Waterhouse & Company aggressively promoted their association with the Countess of Clarendon in stock catalogues and print advertising (see above advertisement) to

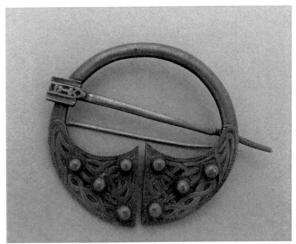

Clarendon Brooch. No marks. Solid cast copper alloy, 3.5 inch diameter, 4.5 inch pin

create a demand for the brooches in the upper echelons of Irish and British society, which would presumably stimulate sales among the middle classes.[20] Waterhouse & Company's strategy proved highly successful and resulted in the sale of more than 2,000 facsimiles of the 'Clarendon' brooch between 1849 and 1852, with demand attributed to the patronage of the Countess of Clarendon.[21] Given the cost, which ranged from 20-30 shillings for a silver version and from four to eight guineas each in gold, such large sales figures demonstrate the impact of viceregal patronage on the Irish facsimile market.[22]

Beginning with the 'Clarendon' brooch, Waterhouse & Company carried out an extensive study of the Irish archaeological jewellery in the Royal Dublin Society, Royal Irish Academy, Trinity College Library and other private collections in 1849 that led directly to the large-scale production of Irish brooches by the firm.[23] The next facsimile of Irish archaeological jewellery issued by Waterhouse & Company was the 'Knight Templar' (Kilmainham) brooch (Fig. 3).[24] The fanciful name given to this design was based on reports that the original brooch was found on the same site in Kilmainham, Co. Dublin where a hospital of the

Fig. 3   Knight Templar Brooch

order of Templars had once stood and was supposedly worn by the Grand Master.[25] The facsimile brooch was a direct copy of a late eighth or early ninth-century lobed penannular brooch in the Royal Irish Academy collection, which was then reduced to approximately half the original size and manufactured in silver, silver gilt or with an oxidised (antique) finish.[26] As with the 'Clarendon' brooch, Joseph Johnson Jr. registered the design for the 'Knight Templar' (Kilmainham) brooch on 25 July 1849, and therefore, may have manufactured the facsimile brooches for retail through Waterhouse & Company.[27]

The unusual 'Arbutus Berry' brooch (Fig. 4), based on a tenth-century silver Viking 'thistle' brooch in the Royal Irish Academy collection, also appeared in 1849. The facsimile brooch was named for the surface texture of the bulbs that decorate the tubular silver ring and the pinhead, which resemble the berries of the Arbutus tree." Waterhouse & Company asserted that the distinctive form of the 'Arbutus Berry' brooch demanded a different approach to production as "the points on the bulbs are too prominent to admit of die work, and, they cannot be made otherwise than by hand."[28] The bulbs on these brooches were cast in solid silver and hand-carved with ridges to create a brambled textural effect.[29]

Waterhouse & Company was not the only Dublin firm active in the production and sale of facsimiles of Irish archaeological jewellery. Edmond Johnson Jr. and other members of his family had been engaged as manufacturers for West & Son for more than forty years, which from 1849 onwards included the production of Irish archaeological-style jewellery.[30] In advance of the royal visit to Dublin, West & Son commissioned Edmond Johnson Jr. to create a brooch as a gift from the Provost and Senior Fellows of Trinity College to Queen Victoria to mark the occasion of

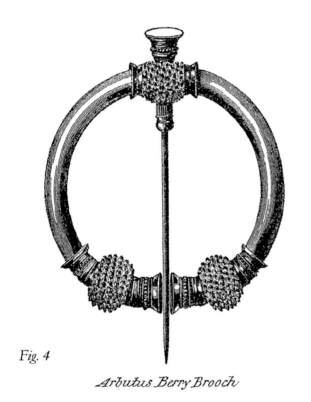

Fig. 4

Arbutus Berry Brooch

her visit to the Library.[31] The model selected for replication was the ninth-century Co. Cavan brooch, a gilt silver brooch with robust cast ornament and tri-lobed bosses decorated with gold filigree and granulation on the terminals and pinhead that could be adapted to hold inset gemstones or pearls.[32] The facsimile brooch produced by Edmond Johnson Jr. was a die-stamped, reduced-size version of the original executed in Wicklow gold with a large Irish river pearl.[33] Thereafter all facsimiles of the Co. Cavan brooch were commonly referred to as the 'Queen's' brooch. Further, during the royal visit to Dublin Prince Albert purchased facsimiles of the 'Arbutus Berry' brooch and the Ballyspellan brooch in silver set with amethysts by Edmond Johnson Jr. for West & Son as gifts for the Queen.[34]

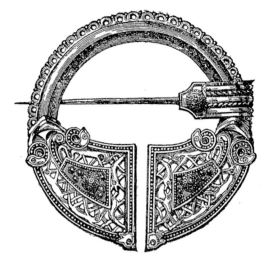

Dublin University Brooch

Fig 5

By early 1850 Waterhouse & Company had expanded their offerings to include the 'University' brooch, a ninth-century silver brooch with a damaged pin found in a Viking cemetery on Rathlin Island, Co. Antrim in the eighteenth century and later owned by Trinity College. The copies of the 'University' brooch (Fig. 5) from Waterhouse & Company were approximately half the size of the original artefact with a reconstructed pin and available in silver, silver gilt or with an oxidised finish.[35] Waterhouse & Company described the ornament on the 'University' brooch as "delicate tracery of which, when closely examined, is found to be formed by the interlacing of the bodies and legs of animals," a feature that clearly identified the original artefact as a distinctive 'type' of ancient Irish brooch representative of a particular stage in the history of Irish jewellery and therefore, ensured its use as a model for facsimiles.[36]

One of the best known, if not *the* most famous, examples of Irish archaeological jewellery brought to light during the nineteenth century was the 'Tara' or 'Royal Tara' brooch, which provided a huge stimulus to the nascent Irish facsimile -

industry. The elaborately ornamented eighth century brooch (Fig. 6) was discovered on a beach near Bettystown, Co. Meath in August 1850.[37] The local woman in possession of the brooch "offered it for sale to the proprietor of an old iron shop in Drogheda, who refused to purchase so light and insignificant an article."[38] Thomas North, a Drogheda watchmaker, ultimately purchased the brooch and in turn sold it later that same year to Samuel S. Waterhouse in Dublin.[39] Waterhouse fabricated the association with the ancient royal site of the Hill of Tara to further increase the value of the brooch by romanticizing its origins. Its designation as the 'Royal Tara' brooch was derived in part from an assertion by the antiquarian and scholar George Petrie, in his paper at the Royal Irish Academy given on 9 December 1850, that a prince or a high-ranking noble had worn it.[40] This royal attribution became even more fitting after the presentation of the original brooch on 20 December 1850 to Queen Victoria and Prince Albert at Windsor Castle and the subsequent royal purchase of two 'Tara' brooch facsimiles (Fig. 7).[41] From 1850 onwards, Waterhouse & Company embarked upon the large-scale, commercial

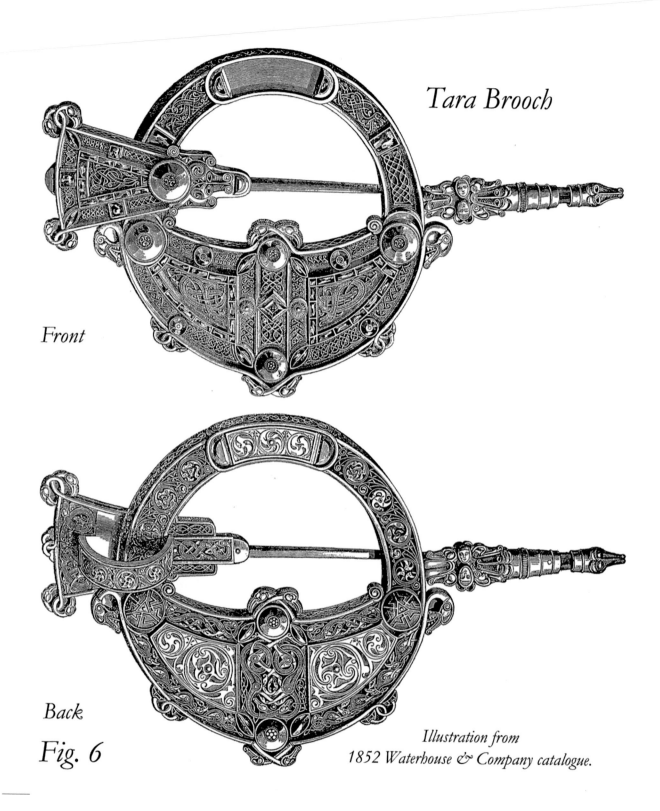

Tara Brooch

Front

Back

Fig. 6

*Illustration from
1852 Waterhouse & Company catalogue.*

production of facsimiles based on the original 'Tara' brooch, which the firm promoted aggressively through patronage, print advertising, stock catalogues and participation at national and international exhibitions, beginning with the 1851 Great Exhibition in London.

The national and international exhibitions held throughout the second half of the nineteenth century were designed to showcase products and industries from around the world and became important platforms for the Irish facsimile industry to gain exposure to new markets. Waterhouse & Company and West & Son participated in the 1851 Great Exhibition in London, the first of the international art and industrial exhibitions, where each firm displayed a wide selection of facsimiles of Irish archaeological jewellery to much acclaim. Both firms received awards for their contributions and a total of seven brooches from Waterhouse & Company and West & Son (likely manufactured by Edmond Johnson Jr.) were singled out for acquisition by the new Museum of Manufactures, later known as the South Kensington Museum and now the Victoria & Albert Museum.[42] The 'Tara' brooch, 'Arbutus Berry' brooch, 'University' brooch and 'Knight Templar' (Kilmainham) brooch were chosen from Waterhouse & Company, along with two facsimiles of the Co. Cavan ('Queen's') brooch and an unidentified brooch design from West & Son, all selected as being representative of distinctive types of Irish brooches.[43] These facsimiles of Irish archaeological jewellery exemplified the principles of good design espoused by the founders of the new museum, which was intended as a resource for students and manufacturers, as well as a vehicle to influence popular consumption.[44]

In 1852 William Acheson exhibited the first facsimiles of the Hunterston brooch at the meeting of the British Association for the Advancement of Science was held at the Belfast

Front of Royal Tara with Catch

Back of Royal Tara with Catch.

Fig.7

Museum, now known as the Ulster Museum, which included an exhibition of Irish antiquities.[45] The late seventh or early eighth-century Irish brooch was named for its association with Hunterston, West Kilbride, Ayrshire in Scotland where it was discovered in 1830.[46] The presence of an inscription on the back face of the brooch inspired its alternative designation as the 'Runic' brooch.[47] The replication of artefacts located outside of Ireland was quite rare and thus, facsimiles of the Hunterston brooch were particularly noteworthy. The choice of the Hunterston brooch as a model was based upon its status as "the most magnificent work of ancient Celtic art that has been found in

Hunterston Brooch. Marked: "Wm Acheson, Dublin". Hollow silver electrotype 2.75 inch maximum diameter.

Scotland", according to a contemporary Scottish commentator, and its visual similarities with the 'Tara' brooch, "which holds a corresponding position among the Celtic antiquities of Ireland".[48]

In the years that followed, facsimiles of Irish archaeological jewellery were well represented at both national and international art and industrial exhibitions. Waterhouse & Company, West & Son, William Acheson and Joseph Johnson Jr. displayed facsimile jewellery at the 1853 Irish Industrial Exhibition in Dublin, where a further three brooches were purchased from the Waterhouse & Company exhibit for the South Kensington Museum in London.[49] The standard repertoire of Irish brooch facsimiles produced by the major firms continued to feature at successive exhibitions in Paris (1855), London (1862) and Dublin (1865). Despite nationalistic references to the facsimile brooches as being distinctively Irish in form, style and manufacture as "worn by the daughters of Erin some centuries ago," these were viewed and understood by visitors primarily as commercial products in the context of promotional events staged to demonstrate progress and innovation in manufacturing, to educate the general public and stimulate trade around the world.[50]

The period between 1840 and 1868 saw the emergence and rapid growth of the Celtic heritage jewellery industry in Dublin, dominated by the mass-production of facsimiles based primarily upon Irish archaeological brooches. A major shift took place after 1868, however, and facsimiles of Irish archaeological jewellery no longer functioned only as commercial products, but also as proxies for the original artefacts, viewed and understood by visitors within the context of a museum display. Several events contributed to this shift, including the creation of an international network for the exchange of reproductions after the 1867 *Exposition Universelle* in Paris, as a response to the demand by

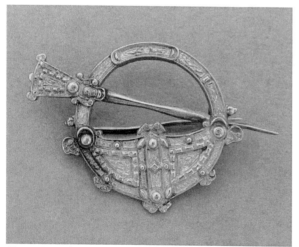

Tara Brooch. Marked "Johnson Ltd. 15Ct. Dublin", Hollow, 1.0625 inch diameter, 1.875 inch pin.

museums for facsimiles of important jewellery and metalwork.[51] In 1868 Waterhouse & Company sold the original 'Tara' brooch to the Royal Irish Academy for £200 on the condition that "it should never be allowed to leave Ireland."[52] In 1868 Joseph Johnson Jr. was chosen to clean and repair the newly discovered Ardagh chalice, which inspired him to move away from reduced-scale facsimile brooches and to manufacture a much wider range of Irish jewellery and metalwork specifically for museums, thereby expanding the market for Irish facsimiles.[53] In contrast, the newly established firm of Hopkins & Hopkins opened in 1868 and devoted a portion of their business to the manufacture of reduced-size facsimiles of well-established and popular Irish brooch designs. By 1868 Edmond Johnson Jr. ceased to operate as manufacturer for West & Son and went on to dominate the Irish facsimile industry in the late nineteenth and early twentieth centuries by producing reduced-scale facsimiles of Irish archaeological jewellery for individual consumers while also making highly accurate facsimiles made to scale for distribution to museums.[54]

The six Dublin firms referenced in this essay are responsible for producing thousands of facsimiles of Irish archaeological jewellery from the 1840s onwards. This jewellery broadly contributed to changing perceptions of Ireland on multiple levels: as commercial products that demonstrated the economic progress made by Ireland; as material evidence of a rich Irish artistic and cultural heritage independent of Great Britain; as souvenirs sold as part of a larger effort to promote Irish tourism; as popular representations that helped to promote and reinforce the status of the original artefacts as Irish national symbols. Most of all, facsimiles of Irish archaeological jewellery are representative of modern advancements celebrated in conjunction with the products and skills of the past.

TK

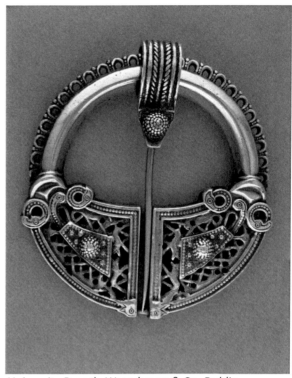

University Brooch. Waterhouse & Co. *Dublin.*
Solid cast silver 2.5 inches diameter

[1] Jeanne Sheehy, *The Rediscovery of Ireland's Past: The Celtic Revival, 1830-1930* (London: Thames and Hudson, 1980), 7; Gabriel Cooney, "Building the Future on the Past: Archaeology and the Construction of National Identity in Ireland," in *Nationalism and Archaeology in Europe*, ed. Margarita Díaz-Andreu García and T. Champion (London: UCL Press, 1996), 148.
[2] Mairead Dunlevy, *Jewellery: 17th to 20th Centuries* (Dublin: National Museum of Ireland, 2001), 16-7; Charlotte Gere and Judy Rudoe, *Jewellery in the Age of Queen Victoria: A Mirror to the World* (London: British Museum Press, 2010), 337, 354 and 376-7.

[3] Douglas Bennett, *Collecting Irish Silver 1637-1900* (London: Souvenir Press, 1984), 95-6 and 157; Charlotte Gere and Hugh Tait, *The Art of the Jeweller: A Catalogue of the Hull Grundy Gift to the British Museum: Jewellery, Engraved Gems, and Goldsmiths' Work* (London: British Museum Publications Limited, 1984), 160; Elizabeth McCrum, "Commerce and the Celtic Revival: Irish Jewelery of the Nineteenth Century," *Éire-Ireland: A Journal of Irish Studies,* 28 (1993), 37; Dunlevy, *Jewellery*, 15-18 and 30.

[4] "Listing of the Principal Goldsmiths of Dublin 1627 to 1800: Abstracted from the Records of the Corporation of Goldsmiths or Guild of All Saints" (National Archives of Ireland, Miscellaneous Index, Document M465); *Thom's Irish Almanac and Official Directory* (Dublin: A. Thom, 1846), 873; Bennett, *Collecting Irish Silver*, 157.

[5] "Dissolution of Partnership," *Freeman's Journal and Daily Commercial Advertiser*, 20 April 1863.

[6] "Law Intelligence," *Freeman's Journal*, 12 December 1854; Bennett, *Collecting Irish Silver*, 145-6 and 57; Cheryl Washer, "The Work of Edmond Johnson: Archaeology and Commerce," in *Imagining an Irish Past: The Celtic Revival, 1840-1940,* ed. T. J. Edelstein (Chicago: David and Alfred Smart Museum of Art, University of Chicago, 1992), 110.

[7] *Thom's Irish Almanac and Official Directory* (Dublin: A. Thom, 1859), 1319; *Thom's Irish Almanac and Official Directory* (Dublin: A. Thom, 1867), 1697; Washer, "The Work of Edmond Johnson," 110.

[8] "Messrs. Hopkins and Hopkins," *Irish Times*, 1 December 1868; *Thom's Irish Almanac and Official Directory* (Dublin: A. Thom, 1869), 1772; Bennett, *Collecting Irish Silver*, 145.

[9] Waterhouse & Company, *Ornamental Irish Antiquities* (Dublin: I. and E. MacDonnell, 1852), 3; Sheehy, *Rediscovery of Ireland's Past*, 86-7; Bennett, *Collecting Irish Silver*, 13-4 and 95-6; McCrum, "Commerce and the Celtic Revival," 37.

[10] Waterhouse & Company, *Ornamental Irish Antiquities*, 3; Patrick F. Wallace and Raghnall Ó Floinn, *Treasures of the National Museum of Ireland: Irish Antiquities* (Dublin: Gill & Macmillan Ltd., 2002), 95-7.

[11] Waterhouse & Company, *Ornamental Irish Antiquities*, 3.

[12] Waterhouse & Company, *Ornamental Irish Antiquities*, 3; Sheehy, *Rediscovery of Ireland's Past*, 87; Bennett, *Collecting Irish Silver*, 13-4; McCrum, "Commerce and the Celtic Revival," 37.

[13] Gere and Judy Rudoe, *Jewellery*, 454-9.

[14] Waterhouse & Company, *Ornamental Irish Antiquities*, 14-5; Bennett, *Collecting Irish Silver*, 95-6; Sheehy, *Rediscovery of Ireland's Past*, 87.

[15] Gere and Tait, *Art of the Jeweller*, 161.

[16] Waterhouse & Company, *Ornamental Irish Antiquities*, 3 and 15-6; McCrum, "Commerce and the Celtic Revival," 42; Gere and Rudoe, *Jewellery*, 448.

[17] McCrum, "Commerce and the Celtic Revival," 37; Clare Philips, *Jewellery from Antiquity to the Present* (London: Thames & Hudson Ltd., 1996), 152; Dunlevy, *Jewellery*, 17.

[18] Philips, *Jewellery from Antiquity*, 152; Bury, *Jewellery*, 539; Dunlevy, *Jewellery*, 17; Gere and Rudoe, *Jewellery*, 450; Gere and Tait, *Art of the Jeweller*, 161.

[19] Waterhouse & Company, *Ornamental Irish Antiquities*, 3 and 15-6.

[20] McCrum, "Commerce and the Celtic Revival," 36-7.

[21] Waterhouse & Company, *Ornamental Irish Antiquities*, 14-5; "The Great Exhibition," *Belfast News-Letter*, 9 June 1851; Sheehy, *Rediscovery of Ireland's Past*, 87.

[22] "The Clarendon Shawl Brooch," *Freeman's Journal*, 11 March 1850; Waterhouse & Company, *Ornamental Irish Antiquities*, 16-7.

[23] Waterhouse & Company, *Ornamental Irish Antiquities*, 3; Bury, *Jewellery*, 537.

[24] "Her Majesty's Goldsmiths: Waterhouse and Company," *Freeman's Journal,* 11 March 1850.

[25] Waterhouse & Company, *Ornamental Irish Antiquities*, 15.

[26] Ibid.

[27] Philips, *Jewellery from Antiquity*, 152; Bury, *Jewellery*, 539; Dunlevy, *Jewellery*, 17; Gere and Rudoe, *Jewellery*, 450; Gere and Tait, *Art of the Jeweller*, 161.

[28] Waterhouse & Company, *Ornamental Irish Antiquities*, 15.

[29] Gere and Rudoe, *Jewellery*, 449.

[30] *Thom's Irish Almanac and Official Directory* (Dublin: A. Thom, 1867), 65; Dunlevy, *Jewellery*, 19; Gere and Rudoe, *Jewellery*, 450.

[31] Dunlevy, *Jewellery*, 50-1.

32 McCrum, "Commerce and the Celtic Revival," 39.

33 Dunlevy, *Jewellery*, 19.

34 Gere and Rudoe, *Jewellery*, 449-50.

35 Ibid.

36 Waterhouse & Company, *Ornamental Irish Antiquities*, 14.

37 Waterhouse & Company, *Ornamental Irish Antiquities*, 7; Niamh Whitfield, "The Finding of the Tara Brooch," *Journal of the Royal Society of Antiquaries of Ireland* 104 (1974): 120-42.

38 Waterhouse & Company, *Ornamental Irish Antiquities*, 7.

39 Whitfield, "Finding of Tara Brooch," 120-1 and 131-7; Douglas Bennett, *Irish Silver* (Dublin: Eason, 1976), 24; Gere and Tait, *Art of the Jeweller*, 160; Nancy Netzer, "Art/Full Ground: Unearthing National Identity and an Early Medieval Golden Age," in *Éire/Land*, ed. V. Kreilkamp (Boston: McMullen Museum of Art, Boston College, 2003), 50.

40 "Royal Irish Academy," *Freeman's Journal*, 11 December 1850; "Royal Irish Academy," *Belfast News-Letter*, 20 December 1850.

41 Waterhouse & Company, *Ornamental Irish Antiquities*, 14; Gere and Tait, *Art of the Jeweller*, 160; Netzer, "Art/Full Ground," 50; Philip McEvansoneya, "The Purchase of the 'Tara' Brooch in 1868, Collecting Irish Antiquities for Ireland," *Journal of the History of Collections* 24, No. 1 (2012): 80-1.

42 Department of Practical Art, *First Report of the Department of Practical Art, Presented to both Houses of Parliament by Command of Her Majesty* (London: George E. Eyre and William Spottiswode for Her Majesty's Stationary Office, 1853), 262; Amy Pierce Miller, "The Selling of Nationalism: The Celtic Revival, Consumerism and the Tara Brooch, 1850-1925" (Master's Thesis, Bard Graduate Center for Studies in the Decorative Arts, Design, and Culture, 2000), 22-3.

43 Ibid.

44 Department of Practical Art, *First Report*, 262; Anthony Burton, *Vision and Accident: The Story of the Victoria and Albert Museum* (London: V&A Publications, 1999), 30.

45 Belfast Natural History and Philosophical Society, *Descriptive Catalogue of the Collection of Antiquities, and Other Objects, Illustrative of Irish History: Exhibited in the Museum, Belfast, on the Occasion of the Twenty-Second Meeting of the British Association for the Advancement of Science, September, 1852* (Belfast: Archer, 1852), 54.

46 Susan Youngs, ed. *The Work of Angels: Masterpieces of Celtic Metalwork, 6th-9th Centuries AD* (London: British Museum Publications in association with the National Museum of Ireland and the National Museums of Scotland, 1990), 91-2.

47 Ibid.

48 "Archaeological Rambles in Argyllshire," *Glasgow Herald,* 3 December 1892.

49 Department of Science and Art, *First Report of the Department of Science and Art* (London: George E. Eyre and William Spottiswode for Her Majesty's Stationary Office, 1854), 241.

50 Anna Jackson, *Expo: International Expositions 1851-2010* (London, V&A Publishing, 2008), 13-5.

51 Department of Science and Art, *Twelfth Report of the Science and Art Department of the Committee of Council on Education* (London: George E. Eyre and William Spottiswode for Her Majesty's Stationary Office, 1865), 23-31; Burton, *Vision and Accident*, 89; Marjorie Trusted, *The Making of Sculpture: The Materials and Techniques of European Sculpture* (London: Victoria & Albert Museum, 2007), 164-5.

52 Royal Irish Academy, "Council Minutes," Vol. 20 (1881-1885), 355-6; Waterhouse & Company, *Antique Irish Brooches*, 7; Whitfield, "The Finding of the Tara Brooch," 138; McEvansoneya, "The Purchase of the 'Tara' Brooch," 77-88.

53 E.R. Windham-Quinn, Earl of Dunraven, "On an Ancient Chalice and Bracelet Lately Found at Ardagh, in the County of Limerick," *Transactions of the Royal Irish Academy* 24 (1873): 435-9.

54 "'The Manufacture of Jewellery in Ireland,'" *Freeman's Journal*, 17 March 1877.

EAST SIDE OF THE SOUTH CROSS, KILKLISPEEN.

Lithograph by Henry O'Neill, *published in his 1857 book*
Illustrations of the Most Interesting of the Sculptured Crosses of Ancient Ireland

The Celtic Cross

The cross with a circle has been popularly known as the "Celtic Cross" since around 1850. The form itself evolved between the 4th and 9th century. Also known as "The Irish Cross" or "The Irish High Cross" this type of cross is now associated with Celtic heritage. Use of the phrase "Celtic Cross" is an acknowledgement that the form is not only Irish, but was and is shared by Scotland, Wales, Cornwall and other regions that were influenced by early Celtic Christianity.

In 1853 casts of several historical High Crosses were exhibited with great success at the Dublin Industrial Exhibition. In 1857 Henry O'Neill published ***Illustrations of the Most Interesting of the Sculptured Crosses of Ancient Ireland.*** These two events stimulated interest in the Celtic Cross as a symbol for a renewed sense of heritage. New versions of the High Cross quickly became fashionable cemetery monuments in Victorian Dublin in the 1860s. From Dublin the revival spread to the rest of the country and beyond.

One of the last surviving circle headed crosses of the medieval tradition is the 15th century *MacLean's Cross* on the Isle of Iona. Decorated with interlaced design this monument and others like it can be said to represent an unbroken tradition that goes back to the earliest days of Christianity in the Celtic lands. From the time of the Protestant Reformation until the Celtic Revival, interlace decoration continued to be used on jewellery, weapons and furniture but appears to have ceased in stone carving. The creation of Celtic crosses almost ceases between 1516 and around 1850.

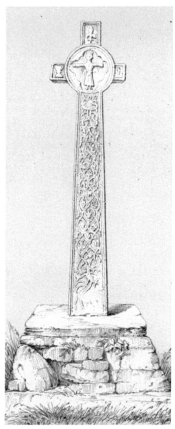

Maclean's Cross, lithograph. Antiquities of Iona *by* Henry Davenport Graham. *Published by Day and Son, London 1850.*

In Scotland, the Celtic cross has reappeared as a jewellery form by 1880. These pendants and brooches were based on the shape of stone monuments. The "Celebrated Iona Cross" on page 36 as well as the pebble cross on page 18 are both early examples. Mairi MacArthur tells of the enterprise named *Iona Celtic Art* begun in 1899 by Alexander and Euphemia beginning on page 39. The Ritchies produced many Celtic crosses as jewelry, wood carvings, embroidery and as table top or alter crosses. The survival of many splendid monuments on Iona served the Ritchies as a pattern book of historical Celtic design.

By the 1890s Celtic crosses began to appear in cemeteries and churches around the world, wherever there was a Scottish or Irish Diaspora population with pride in their origins. Irish cemeteries now seem to be choked with Celtic cross monuments. Inspection of the

Advertisement on the back cover of Royal Tourist Guides Iona & Staffa, 1882.

"The Celebrated Iona Cross" Silver and shell brooch. John M'Gilvray, Oban. The lozenge mark on the back indicates design registration for 1883.

dates inscribed on them shows few are more than 100 years old. Most of the elaborate crosses erected in Ireland prior to 1900 marked the graves of priests. After Irish independence a flood of Celtic cross monuments appear and the majority of the crosses seen today are from the 20th century.

Celtic Revival crosses are often decorated with Celtic interlace and other antique decoration but they are also frequently decorated with contemporary religious and national symbols. Harps and shamrocks decorate many of the earlier Celtic Revival examples. Sacred Hearts, messages such as "Rest in Peace" or "IHS" monograms are also evidence that these monuments were not merely imitations of historical sculpture, but have become a traditional form for expressing conventional fashions and sentiments.

In Ireland the majority of Celtic Crosses are created for Catholic patrons, but the Protestant Church of Ireland uses the Celtic Cross as well. Many other Protestants of Celtic heritage, especially those outside Ireland, also make use of the Celtic Cross. The Moderator of the Presbyterian Church USA has, as an emblem of his office, a silver pectoral Celtic Cross that was acquired on Iona in 1946. The American Presbyterians have used the Celtic cross as a logo for many years, reflecting that denomination's historical connection to the Church of Scotland.

The symbolic significance of the circle has been the subject of much speculation. Folklore often endows the circle with a message of eternity, as a circle has no beginning or end. Alternatively the circle may represent a halo and convey a message of blessedness. Associations with Sun symbolism has been frequently suggested, as well as finding origins in the laurel wreaths of Roman imperial monograms or the Egyptian Ankh symbol. The very popular notion that there are pagan origins resonated with Celtic Revival beliefs that Celtic art was a pure native tradition. This point of view was strenuously argued by Henry O'Neill, although it was rejected by the more conventional scholars.

The shape of the negative space in the "arm pits" between the central intersection and the inside of the circle are frequently key-hole shaped on Celtic Revival crosses. This shape is occasionally seen in medieval versions, such as the Kilklispeen cross on page 23, however on most medieval crosses the negative space is smaller and formed of two arcs. Pictish cross slabs tend to have four arcs that form not a perfect circle, but more of a squared cushion. The "Celebrated Iona Cross" on the previous page illustrates both of these peculiarities.

The Celtic cross is now one of the most popular emblems of Celtic design. The trend has gone from the impressive monuments of the early Celtic Revival, that like their medieval prototypes, were public statements of the art of the community, to rendering of the Celtic cross for personal expression of faith and heritage. Jewellery has replaced grave stones as the most common expression of this symbol. Craft objects for personal use, clothing and tattoos are all media where new versions of the Celtic cross are evolving in the continuum of this powerful symbol. *SAW*

Kildalton Cross, 2 inches long, die-struck 9 ct gold. The dies for this pendant were made for Scotia Jewellery *in Dunoon in the 1970s, later manufactured by* Angus Milne *of Salen Silver on the Isle of Mull.*

CATHEDRAL. EAST FRONT
IONA.

Alexander and Euphemia Ritchie in the garden of Shuna Cottage, Iona, with their dogs Kim and Fifie.

Iona Celtic Art

E. Mairi MacArthur

Just over one hundred years ago, at the official Census of 1911, 222 people lived on Iona, approximately twice the number of permanent residents there today. The mix of occupations recorded was typical of a small island community: farmers, ploughmen, fishermen, sailors, a weaver, a joiner, a dressmaker, a grocer or two, a postmaster. Two households, however, stand out. Indeed, these Census entries were unique in the Scottish Highlands of a century ago: at Shuna Cottage, Alexander Ritchie, occupation Art Metal Work; his wife Euphemia Ritchie, Designer in Celtic Work. And along the street, at Staffa Cottage, was James Thomson, Celtic Art Worker.

This was a local business, already established for over a decade, and its name was *Iona Celtic Art*. The hundreds of visitors who flocked from the steamships sailing out of Oban every summer knew it well, as did many who wrote about the island. For example, the naturalist Seton Gordon, in his book *Highways & Byways in the West Highlands*, published in 1935:

> In any account of Iona the name of Mr. Alexander Ritchie cannot be passed over, for besides having unrivalled knowledge of the old history of the island, he has created the industry of copying (mostly in silver) the ancient Celtic designs. The work, which is highly skilled, enables the present generation to appreciate Early Celtic craftsmanship.

And in 1941, the poet and playwright Gordon Bottomley penned a lengthy tribute to the Ritchies in *The Scots Magazine*. They had died in January that year but the national press, Bottomley felt, had not given them their proper due, owing perhaps to the dominance of War news. For him they had been both 'faithful friends' and 'among the island notables of the time'. And he went on:

> The wide-spread success of their jewellery and table-silver can well be a lasting memorial to their life and work together...
> Almost to the end they would have a new design or two in hand.
> ... Many besides myself will find Iona almost unthinkable without Alexander Ritchie.

Abbott MacKinnon's Cross, 15th century monument, illustrated in __Antiquities of Iona__ by Henry Davenport Graham. Published by Day and Son, London 1850.

Iona Galley Shield brooch, Hand engraved, probably from a drawing design by Alexander and Euphemia Ritchie *of Iona. Silver,1.125 x 1.575 inches. Hallmark "CS*FS" Chester 1905-06.*

Even my generation, brought to Iona as children for summer holidays from the 1950s, and who therefore never met the Ritchies ,have alwaysbeen familiar with their name and with their work. In every island house there was an embroidered cushion or a brass ashtray or a silver tea-caddy spoon. These were not display curios, kept behind glass, but items in everyday use. Brooches, chains, hatpins and kiltpins were also worn regularly, not just for special occasions.

Alexander Ritchie was born in 1856 in Tobermory, Mull, where his father was a steamship captain. The Ritchies had moved around the Scottish coast, from a Buchan fishing village in the north to the mouth of the River Ayr and then to the Kintyre peninsula in the far south-west. In 1868 the family moved to from Mull to Iona, to lease the St Columba Hotel and farm. Alec was then 12 years old and a native Gaelic speaker. As a young man he trained as a marine engineer and sailed with the British India Steam Shipping Company for nearly 20 years, until a shipwreck in the West Indies forced early retirement; a leg injury left him with a permanent limp. Back home on Iona in the early 1890s, he gained seasonal employment from the Duke of Argyll, as guide to the summer visitors. In 1899, when ownership of the historic sites passed from the Duke to the new Iona Cathedral Trust, the appointment of official Guide and Custodian was confirmed.

Sometime in the 1890s two junior draughtsmen with the Glasgow firm of architects, Honeyman & Keppie, were sent to Iona to help with survey work at the Cathedral. They were Charles Rennie Mackintosh and James Herbert NacNair. Did Alec Ritchie show them around the buildings? He had such a keen interest in the monuments that some lengthy conversations were at least highly likely. And was this, perhaps, the personal contact that gave Alec the idea of enrolling for classes in metalwork at Glasgow School of Art? We don't know, but this he began to do, in the winter months, at the age of nearly 40 years. In Glasgow Alec met a fellow mature student, Euphemia Thomson, who was taking classes in embroidery. Euphemia had been born in 1862 in Argyll and her childhood was spent partly on the isle of Shuna, south of Oban, where her father had tenancy of a farm. We do not know what led *her* to the Glasgow School of Art in her early 30s. But she was probably already handy with a needle and the excitement around the growing Arts & Crafts Movement, and the Celtic Revival, inspired many young women to take up classes in applied arts. And the embroidery department at the Glasgow School of Art, headed by Jessie Newbury, was particularly innovative and attractive.

In 1898 the couple married in Glasgow and set up home on Iona, naming their house Shuna Cottage. By the following year they had a workshop behind the house and a sales hut inside the grounds of the ruined medieval Nunnery. They never lost the link with Glasgow, however, returning there for a spell each winter and this kept them in touch with artistic activity in the city. From a note in a book about the firm Keppie Design, we know that Alec joined the Glasgow Archaeological Society in 1906, with the encouragement of architect John Honeyman, who had been closely involved in repairs to Iona Cathedral.

Iona Galley shield brooch cast from a chased model. Silver, 1.125 x 1.575 inches. Hallmarked "AR" "IONA" Chester 1911-12. Most Ritchie jewellery was manufactured by casting from chased models for the remainder of his career.

Contemporaries must have been aware of what the Ritchies were doing; an illustrated article from *The Art Journal* of 1907 praised their originality:...the work of Mrs. Ritchie, based on the splendid interlacing patterns of ancient Celtic art, may also be instanced as an example of another ideal of embroidery than that of the School of Art. The decorative metal work of Mr Ritchie has the same source as this embroidery, a source that is not in the text book of design but in individual study of the lovely work that is to be found where the carvers of stone wrought out the intricacies of their art.

Years later, Alec was to write to a friend that he had set out 'on very little except hope but...my wife being an expert with the pencil, we began to adapt the Iona designs to silver and have had as much success as I can expect'. This seems a modest assessment of such a varied range of products, all made to a high standard. Photographs of the shop's interior show walls and cases crammed with beaten brass and copper, chased silverware, mirrors, picture frames, decorated boxes, trays, chalices, jugs, spoons, enamelled jewellery, patterned bags, carved wooden or marble crosses.

The sources of inspiration among which Alec Ritchie had grown up are immediately apparent: the knotwork, spirals and entwined animal forms on Early Christian crosses and on the columns of the Abbey Church; the foliage, interlace and galleys on the graveslabs of the medieval Highland chiefs. The couple were also keenly interested in the illuminated manuscripts of the Columban monasteries, and in the Pictish stone patterns. A list of books from Shuna Cottage has survived, confirming their archaeological and historical interests. It includes, for example, James Drummond's *Sculptured Monuments in Iona and the West Highlands* (1881) and Sir Edward Sullivan's illustrated description of *The Book of Kells* (1915).

*Cigarette case, chased with galley and knotwork Silver 3.5 x 2.75 inches. Hallmark "AR", "Iona", "CS*FS", Birmingham 1908-09. The multiple marks are a clear indication of Ritchie's early collaboration with the London firm of Cornelius Saunders and Francis Shepard, who manufactured in Birmingham and Chester*

*Pictish Penannular brooch, Silver, 2.5 inch diameter. Hallmark "CS*FS", Chester 1903-04*

One summer a young visitor begged Mr Ritchie to make her a silver hairband. He copied the foliage design on a fillet, or medieval hair ornament, which had been unearthed during work on Iona Nunnery in 1923. He made a bangle with the same pattern and he reproduced to scale a finely worked medieval silver spoon, which became one of his most popular items. Author Charles Cammell, in a book entitled *Heart of Scotland*, described these Nunnery finds which also included a gold ring with a rope pattern and added that, when he married in 1932, he gave his bride an exact replica 'made specially for me, of the purest gold, by Ritchie, the renowned silversmith of Iona'.

So, commissions or one-off special items were definitely part of the business of Iona Celtic Art: as a wedding gift; a retirement presentation; a decorated leather binding for a bible; a pendant setting for an Iona greenstone. In 1926, Mrs Nicolson, wife of the then Secretary of the Gaelic Society of Inverness, was presented with a chased silver cup made by Mr Ritchie. In 1929, a newspaper report stated that Lady Haig, widow of Commander Haig, opened Bunessan Hall on the Ross of Mull and was given a Celtic brooch specially designed by Mrs Ritchie, Iona. Bigger commissions included memorial brass plaques by Alec Ritchie in several churches in Argyll - plus the one for Lady Victoria Campbell in Crown Court Church of Scotland in London - and two splendid silver shields for An Comunn Gaidhealach, prizes at the National Mod. These are still competed for each year.

The group of Nunnery finds was taken to the National Museum of Scotland but plenty of other inspiration remained on the island. One favourite, which the Ritchies adapted in several ways, was the late 15th century MacKinnon's Cross. Its griffin, with the tail merging into a plant scroll, was used on trays, vases, candle-sconces and on a planter. Hugely varied use was made of the leaf patterns found on much of the Iona stonework, and of the galley, resonant of the island's past history and of its continuing links with the sea.

Euphemia taught embroidery and leather tooling to many of the island girls but more formal apprentices and outworkers became essential quite early on, so successful was the business. One was Helen MacPhail, born in 1905. From childhood she had a displaced hip and there was some concern about finding for her a not too strenuous occupation. The training she received from the Ritchies, and in Glasgow where they sent her, suited her well. She became very skilled and many of her brass pieces and paper patterns have been preserved. Helen remained on Iona all her life, latterly helping a sister and brother in the Post Office which also, for a time, sold Celtic Art souvenirs.

James Thomson, mentioned in the 1911 Census, continued to produce brass items for the Ritchies even after he returned to Glasgow. Iain MacCormick, born on Iona in 1917, had his first lessons in metalworking as a boy in Alec's workshop. After school he went to agricultural college but, following War service, he helped train disabled ex-servicemen in Celtic metalwork and later became a teacher of technical subjects in Paisley. In his spare time he built up a business as a silversmith and draughtsman of Celtic design. His meticulous notebooks and artwork survive, as does a huge array of brass, copper, silver and marble items made in the tradition of the Ritchies but often with Iain's own original adaptation. Among his work books was a copy of George Bain's classic manual, *Celtic Art the methods of construction*. For many years Iain's mother, Hannah, ran the Highland Home Industries shop on Iona which inherited both the site and the stock of Iona Celtic Art after the Ritchies died.

Miniature silver crosses set in green Iona marble. 3.75 inch high. On the left is MacLean's Cross Based on the 15th century stone monument on Iona. (Pg 35) On the right is Saint Martin's Cross, which is copied from the 8th century high cross. Both bear hallmarks: "ICA" , "AR" "IONA" Birmingham 1936-37". These same crosses were made as jewellery also.

Prioress Anna Brooch, silver, 1.75 inch diameter. Hallmarks: "IONA" "AR" Glasgow 1934-35.

Brass buckle, unmarked and never finished, with the chaser's pitch still on the back. 2.5 x 3.75 inch.

Iain died in 1998. A year before, he had gifted to a younger relative, the artist Mhairi Killin, masters for a range of Ritchie silver pieces. This was to give her new island craft business, now Aosdana Gallery, a solid start and to ensure a continuing tradition of Celtic art on Iona. The gallery is in the refurbished steadings of the Columba farm, where the young Alec Ritchie will undoubtedly have helped milk the cows or played. So a circle has been nicely completed.

In 1937 some Ritchie jewellery pieces were included in a three-day Scottish Industries Exhibition in London and one of the organisers, Jean Bruce of the Highland Home Industries, described Mr Ritchie as 'one of her finds'. It seems a late date to be 'found' as he was already over 80 years. Yet it is true that the Ritchies neither exhibited, nor promoted, their work particularly widely on the mainland. On the other hand, each summer the world came to them. In their home the couple entertained a stream of artists, writers, clergymen, professors and artistocracy and in their shop they built friendships with many regular customers. They were undoubtedly widely known and respected in their lifetime. It was in the years following that, somehow, there seemed to be no easy means to extend their reputation beyond the island. And so, in the world of museums, art and antiques - with a few exceptions - their name and reputation was not at all well known through the middle decades of the 20th century. A collector of Keswick School metalware, in Cumbria, remained baffled for years by the maker's mark on a brass candle sconce which he read as a single, mysterious name: ARIONA. Until my own book about Iona Celtic Art came out, he was quite unaware of the mark AR IONA for Alexander Ritchie.

The Ritchies had no children and the wider family became quite scattered. Bill Hope, who lived in South Africa, wrote to me after the publication of my book. His great-grandmother was Isabella Ritchie, Alec's oldest sister.

I just wish my mother could have seen this book. It would have been a great delight to her. She had met Uncle Alec on several occasions and had quite a collection of his items and often used to talk about him and Aunt Effie - and I always had the feeling that she thought they had not received due recognition. I am sure there were others in the family who felt the same. Now, 60 years later, that has been remedied.

Silver and enamel dove pendant. 2 x 1.5 inch. Marked: "AR" and "IONA", no assay or date.

And in her book *Hand, Heart and Soul. The Arts and Crafts Movement in Scotland*, Elizabeth Cumming describes the Ritchies' enterprise as 'a key example of dedication to craft mixed with small-scale entrepreneurship'. Alec Ritchie may not have set out to earn a living from his own handiwork; only by chance did he leave his chosen profession, the sea. Yet what he and Euphemia achieved was new and original work, rooted in the old, across a range of media, of dazzling variety, of practical use and of great beauty. They were keen to hand on their skills and were to the end actively involved in many aspects of island life.

A small timber-panelled room above the Abbey Cloisters looks out onto the Sound of Iona. This is now a library, its first books and initial funding bequeathed by Alec and his brother, the Reverend Robert L. Ritchie. Above the door is an instruction which, happily, is now being fulfilled by events such as this exhibition and by today's Celtic craftsmen and women in Scotland and abroad:

Remember Alexander Ritchie, for many years custodian of this Abbey, and his wife Euphemia Catherine Thomson, who together revived the Celtic arts and crafts on this island.

EMM

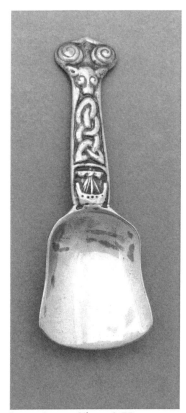

Sugar Spoon Silver, 3.75 x 1.25 inch. Marked "IONA" Birmingham hallmarks for 1936-37.

Iain McCormick, Malachy Gormley, and a disabled British veteran of WWII, at work in Celtic Art Industries, Glasgow, Scotland, late 1940's. Two rare reference books are visible under the bench. The Early Christian Monuments of Scotland *by Allen and Anderson 1905 and* The Sculptured Stones of Scotland *by John Stuart 1856. Copyright: The Iain McCormick Archive, Groam House Museum Collection and the Iain McCormick Estate.*

Plaid brooch, cast, silver and smoky quartz 1.875 inch diameter. Hallmarked "DB" for Dawson-Bowman. Edinburgh assay for 1975

Ritchie design brooch, detail from MacLean's Cross marked "IMC STERLING SCOTLAND"

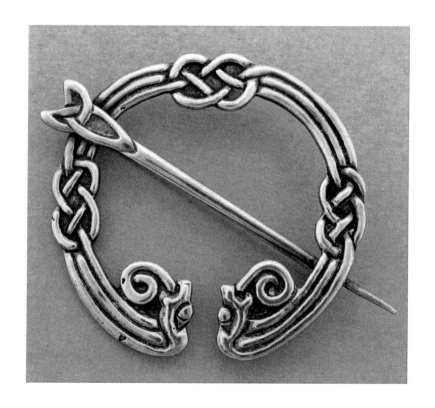

Penannular Brooch original design by Iain McCormick marked "IMC IONA STERLING SCOTLAND"

Penannular Brooch, silver hallmarked "RA, Edinburgh 1971-72"
The mark "RA" has caused some confusion in 20th century Scottish jewellery since it is the reverse of Alexander Ritchie's "AR" mark. "RA" is the mark used by Glasgow Highland outfitter Robert Allison, whose jewellery often imitated the Iona style.

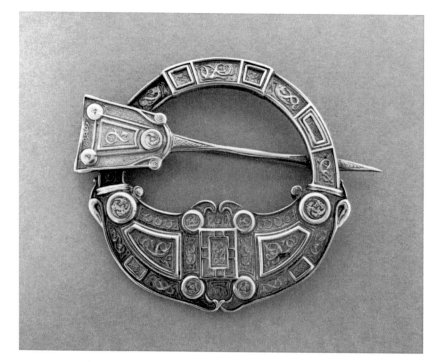

Hunterston Brooch, cast silver. 2.75 inch diameter. Celtic Art Ltd., The model for this piece, which is still in production, was an Acheson electrotype from the previous century. Edinburgh hallmarks, "CA" 1975.

"Iona" Wedding Ring, John Hart. In 1957 The Iona Shop in the Argyll Arcade, Glasgow began offering this ring. For many years it was the only continuous Celtic knot ring on the market. The interwoven, endless knot theme of the design is a natural complement to the symbolic function of the wedding ring, which as a circle has no beginning or end, so it is a symbol of never-ending love. The very style of a Celtic ring is also an emblem of heritage, affirmations of which are expressed as the family connects the traditions of past with the future that a marriage anticipates.

John Hart was one of the first Celtic jewelers to switch from sand casting to modern lost-wax casting, that borrowed technology from dentistry. This method of manufacturing multiples was much more practical for finger rings. This simple and basic ring design was a watershed breakthrough that foreshadowed the shift from brooches as the primary form of Celtic jewellery to rings, which since the 1990s have become very popular.

Citrine silver brooch, marked "IONA" JH for John Hart and Edinburgh hallmarks for 1965. John Hart was one of the original craftsmen hired by Hamish Dawson-Bowman at Celtic Art Industries in 1946. Hart was an engraver. After he began to cast multiples of his designs by means of lost-wax models reproduced in rubber molds he discovered that this technique lent itself well to making perforated interlaced designs which were much more difficult to reproduce using the sand casting method that had been formerly used. Many of his earlier designs were re-mastered by piercing out the background. While this development is not original to Hart, it was a style that worked so naturally with interlaced designs that it gradually became the most common way to use interlace in jewelry. The Iona Shop in Glasgow, which was begun in 1947 and expanded to Oban in 1966, bought all of John Hart's output after he left CAI and worked on his own until 1979. Then Hart's son, also named John, took over the jewellery business and moved it from Glasgow to South Uist in the Outer Hebrides, where it continues as "Hebridean Jewellery".

Kilt Pins

The use of Highland weaponry as the motif for kilt pins began with Victorian pebble jewellery and continued with the Iona tradition in cast silver. The now common claymore sword with a circular "targe" shield appears to have been a Ritchie variation.

Galley and triquetra knot kilt pin 2.5 inch long.
Marked "SILVER IONA".
Claymore and targe kilt pin, 2.5 inch long.
Marked "S&Co" Chester 1951-52

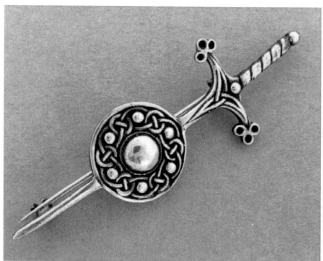

Claymore and targe kilt pin, John Hart. 2.5 inch long.
Glasgow hallmarks for 1962-63 "JH IONA"

Highland Outfitters, that sell kilts and accessories, were a major outlet for Celtic jewellery in the 20th century. These merchants would also sell jewellery that is traditionally worn with Highland dress, but does not have its origin in the traditions of Celtic art. The cap badge, that is frequently perceived as "Celtic" by this association, conventionally features the heraldic crest from a clan chief's coat of arms or a similar emblem of a Scottish regiment. This is typically supported in a circular buckled garter emblazoned with the chief's motto. The Scottish court of Lord Lyon King of Arms has legal jurisdiction over heraldic property, which also includes tartans.

Clan Elliot cap badge, silver. 1.575 inch diameter. Thomas Ebbutt, hallmarked "TE" with Edinburgh marks for 1957-58.

Sleipnir brooch, this eight-legged charger is the chosen mount for Odin, chief of the Norse gods. Jack Rae, Shetland Jewellery, silver, 1.5 inch diameter. Edinburgh hallmarks 1963-64.

Jack Rae trained as a jeweler in Edinburgh. In 1945 he and his wife Margaret moved to the Shetland Islands where they established Shetland Silvercraft in 1953. Specializing in Celtic and Norse themed designs, the business continues as Shetland Jewellery under the management of Jack's son Kenneth Rae.

Ola Gorie at the bench in the late 1960s. Ola was the first jewellery graduate from Gray's School of Art in Aberdeen in 1960. This photo was taken in the late 1960s when she had returned to Orkney to establish her business after a Canadian sojourn. The success of her business was followed by a number of other jewellery enterprises in the Orkney Islands that ranged in size from individual craftsmen to fairly large manufacturers.

Ola Gorie Jewellery

Silver Pictish Brooch based on the crescent and V-rod symbol that frequently is found in the early medieval art of Northeast Scotland. The Pictish culture stretched from the Firth of Forth to the Shetland Islands in the 4th to 10th centuries. Hallmarks: "OMG" Edinburgh 1970-71. 1.75 x 1.25 inches.

Coppergate Brooch, Silver, design circa 1975. Adapted from the nose piece of an Anglo-Saxon helmet found in York. The interlace of this piece was sculpted by assembling individually crafted components to make a three dimensional model for casting. 2.75 x 1.25 inches.

Nouveau Thistle brooch. 18 carat gold. 1990s design. 2.25 x 0.6 inches.

Tri-Dragon brooch, Tain Silver, Douglas and Rita Scott.
Hallmarks: "RS" Edinburgh 1990.
2 x 2.12 inches.

The Claddagh Ring

The Claddagh Ring has its roots in a type of finger ring called *Fede* or faith ring. Since Roman times these consisted of clasped hands and often worked as a pair of two intertwined rings with a hand on each that would slide together. Worn as a sign of devotion to a spouse or beloved, this widespread European jewellery tradition evolved a peculiar variation in the West of Ireland that has come to be known as the Claddagh Ring. The hands clasp a heart in the manner of presentation with a crown over the heart.

By tradition, a Claddagh Ring is passed from mother to her eldest daughter. The manner in which it is worn indicates the status of the wearer. On the right hand with the heart worn outwards it indicates that the wearer is single and available for courtship. Worn on the ring finger of the left hand with the heart outwards it shows that the heart is occupied, but not yet married. Worn on the left ring finger with the heart facing inwards the Claddagh Ring declares that the wearer is married. Tradition also holds that the three motifs of the ring are symbolic, the heart for love, the crown for loyalty and the hands for friendship.

There are two legends about the origin of the Claddagh ring. Both involve members of the Joyce tribe. One Margaret Joyce married a wealthy Spanish trader, Domingo de Rona. After his death she inherited his fortune and remarried Oliver Og French, the Mayor of Galway 1596-7. Margaret was renowned for her charity and for building a great number of bridges at her own expense. One day an eagle flying overhead dropped a golden ring into her bosom, set with a rare and unknown stone. This miracle was seen as a reward from Heaven for Margaret's good works. The ring became the model for the Claddagh Ring.

Traditional Claddagh Ring, 9 ct. gold. Dublin hallmarks for 1983. Maker's mark "TB".

The second and more widely known legend is that Richard Joyce was captured by Algerian Corsairs around 1675. Enslaved, he was purchased by a Moorish goldsmith, who trained him in the craft. In 1689 King William III sent an ambassador to Algeria to demand the release of any and all British subjects who were enslaved in that country, which at the time would have included the Irish. His forceful negotiations were successful. The master of Richard Joyce had grown very fond of him and begged that he remain with him in freedom, going so far as to offer Joyce his only daughter's hand in marriage and half his property. Joyce refused the offer and returned to Galway, where he successfully followed the trade he had learned in his captivity. In the more romantic versions of the tale he marries the sweetheart that faithfully waited fourteen years for him. The earliest Claddagh Ring examples that can be reliably dated do, in fact, bear the mark of goldsmith Richard Joyce, who was active in Galway circa 1689-1737.

Claddagh Rings were very commonly used in the area around Galway since the late 17th century. The Claddagh is a fishing village on the outskirts of Galway City. It was a local fashion, which although it began to get wider notice in the early 20th century, was never really a part of the Celtic Revival. Towards the end of the 20th century there was an explosion of interest in the Claddagh Ring, both as jewellery and as an icon of Irishness that now adorns many other objects from pub signs to grave stones. In more recent years it has been embellished with interlace designs and combined with other Celtic and Irish symbols, but this is a very recent phenomenon that corresponds with the worldwide expansion in popularity of the Claddagh ring as an emblem of Irish identity.   *SAW*

Garda cap badge. Stamped base metal, electroplated. 3 inches wide. 20th century. Garda Síochána na hÉireann, literally "Guardians of the Peace of Ireland" is the Irish police force. The design, lettering and detail of the emblem of the Garda all derive from very traditional Celtic art prototypes. After Irish independence in 1921 the public fashion for Celtic design in jewellery quickly faded. However, just as Irish Gaelic was made the official language of the state, the Celtic style did persist for official public emblems, monuments and documents.

Gaelic Athletic Association (GAA) Gaelic Football medal made by the Jewellery and Metal Company, Dublin. Sterling silver and enamel. 1 .25 inch. Hallmarked for 1958 and engraved "G.A.A. Mid. W. Div. 1961. Champions A League". The GAA was founded in 1884 with one of its stated purposes to "foster a spirit of earnest nationality" and the organization was closely aligned with the struggle for independence. During the Irish War of Independence in 1920 "Black and Tans", an irregular British auxiliary force, entered Croke Park in Dublin during a GAA football match, on what came to be remembered as "Bloody Sunday". As reprisal for the IRA assassinations of a group of British Intelligence officers earlier that day, they fired indiscriminately into the crowd, killing 13 and wounding nearly a hundred spectators and athletes. In the middle of the 20th century Celtic ornament lost much of the popularity that had been attained earlier in the century in Ireland, but remained in use for purposes where it had been institutionalized such as government documents, currency design, GAA regalia and Irish dance costume. This example was a prize for an American branch of the GAA and is more substantial than what would have typically been awarded at a similar level in Ireland. Marks and engraving on the back can be seen on page 69.

Aidan Breen, Swords, County Dublin

The red material is chaser's pitch, which is used to hold sheet metal for chasing and reposee work. Designs are punched into the metal using blunt chisels. The pitch supports the work as it is modeled sculpted in relief.

Early Days in the Silver Trade
My Memories
Aidan Breen

Mr. Barnes got me my first job in M.H.Gill & Sons, Printers, Publishers, and Ecclessticial Art Metal Works at 56 Upper O'Connell Street Dublin. It was the summer of 1959 and I was 14 years of age. Mr. Barnes or Ted as he was known to his peers, was an English Catholic who came to Ireland after World War II. He was a friend of my aunt Bridie. And he was a great friend and mentor to me in Gill's.

While the Gills shop fronted onto O'Connell Street, the workshops were in Moore Lane at the back of the shop. The printing activity took place directly behind the shop while the building that housed the foundry, the carpentry & picture framing workshops, plus the silver shop was a little further down the lane from the printers. Across the lane was the brass shop that employed about thirty craftsmen and women. The brass shop manufactured altar railings, altar candlesticks, tabernacles, sanctuary lamps, thuribles for incense and candle shrine holders and a host of other liturgical articles.

I was based in the silver shop and swept the floors first thing every morning. My next job was to get the men in both the brass shop and silver shop their cakes and cigarettes and whatever else they needed. When this was done all of us who worked in the silvershop knelt down and said a decade of the rosary. After we said the rosary I made the tea for our 10 o'clock break.

The silver shop employed four silversmiths and an apprentice, a chaser, a polisher and a silver/ gold plater. In the small office attached to the workshop worked Mr. Barnes and Mary Cleary.

Mary was a burnisher. Her job entailed burnishing the gold plating on the sacred vessels with steel and agate tools and a soapy water solution. This made the gold gleam and also helped to give the gilding the capacity to stand up to the wear and tear that the liturgical vessels would be subjected to. Her father was the foreman of the silver shop and her brother John was also one of the silversmiths. Every item made in the silver shop was formed by hand raising, which means it was hammered up from sheet.

The silvershop produced altar plate for use in the sacramental life of the Catholic Church. They included chalices for celebrating the Eucharist and ciboriums and patens for the distribution of Holy Communion. Monstrance's for the exposition of the Blessed Sacrament in Benediction. Also pyxes for carrying the holy communion and stocks for the holy oils used for anointing the sick and dying and other blessings.

The repertoire of motifs in use in the workshop that were either engraved or chased on the altar plate included; Celtic interlacing, the Wheat and Vine, the Pelican feeding her young by piercing her breast and feeding them her blood, the Lamb, the PAX sign, the Alpha & Omega, the IHS and of course the Cross in all its manifestations. All these symbols were akin to musical notes and were used in many different combinations to produce different designs to embellish the chalices and Monstrance's and other sacred vessels.

At this time in Ireland, and especially Dublin, a lot of new churches were being built to serve the new parishes growing up in the expanding suburbs.

Moore Lane, Dublin Gills silver shop was located on the right.

The architects who designed the churches also designed the church furnishings including the liturgical vessels.

Gills were famous for its Papal DeBurgo Chalice that was presented to Pope Pius XII in 1950 by Sean O'Kelly, President of Ireland. It was in the style of the famous DeBurgo-O'Malley chalice made in 1494. The liner was chased with a mixture of pure Celtic peltra motifs and interlacing. The rest of the chalice was chased all over with the combinations of designs mentioned above. It was fabricated out of 18ct gold. Gills also made a bronze Monstrance for the newly opened Telefís Eireann (Irish National Television) for the televised Benediction program. It was in the shape of a Celtic cross with flat chased interlacing covering the four surfaces of the cross. It was made of bronze and not highly polished because they did not want too much reflection from the television studio lights.

When proposals for new jobs arrived in the workshop, the foreman, George Cleary, would gather the other silversmiths, the polisher, Christy Edwards, and the chaser Bobby McGrath. This conference took place at a sturdy table where the drawings for all new work were first evaluated for pricing and to examine the feasibility of making

the article. I can still see and hear in my mind the great discussions that took place at the table. One comment in particular still sticks in my mind. "Ah sure, you could not make this. These architects know nothing about silversmithing." This table was also the place where every item made in the workshop was given the once over to make sure everything was as it was supposed to be. The table was perfectly level and a plum bob hung from the ceiling to make sure the article was straight.

It was also my job to bring and collect work from the out-workers and specialist craftsmen and women scattered across the city. There were three different engravers used by Gills. Also a jewel case maker by the name of Jack Barclay, who custom made cases for the chalices, ciboriums and monstrances I brought to him. I loved going over to his workshop, where he would tell me to sit down and rest while he took measurements of the item. Then he would tell me stories of his time in the First World War, when he served with the Black Watch, a Scottish regiment. He also told me stories from *The Táin* and of CúChulainn's amorous adventures with the opposite sex which he said they did not mention in the schools we all went to. The Dublin Assay Office was another port of call where I brought the silverware over in a green baize sack. The Assay Office is where all items of silver and gold manufactured in Ireland must by law be tested and hallmarked before they can be offered for sale.

We would get the odd order for a Bishops Pectoral cross which would be studded with jewels and sometimes other articles could be gem set. These articles would be sent out to John Colgan the stone setter. The Pectoral Cross was the nearest we came to making jewellery. As at that time in the precious metal trade silversmiths did not make jewellery. A jeweller would have been called a goldsmith. Although silversmiths also worked in gold, the term goldsmith means in this sense someone who makes small work.

I helped around all the workshops and in the office. Mr. Barnes would get me to make new drawings of the various articles that were made in the workshop. I would pumice the brass hammered patens in the polishing shop to get the marks and scratches out, and scratch brush newly plated items.

John Wills was the picture framer. I would touch up any of the frames that were damaged in the making, using oil paints. I was good at this. John was the first man I met who had ever been to Spain. He would regale me in words about the deeds and dramas of the bull fighters and the flamenco dancers he saw there.

Billy Dunne was the carpenter and the odd time I would go out on a job with him. Billy was one of the most intelligent, if not *the* most intelligent man, I have met in my life. He was, as they say, "out in 16" (he took part in the 1916 Rising as a young messenger). He was a bagpiper and a fluent Irish speaker. Before Google, everybody from high up to low down, who had an unanswered question went to Billy for the answer, which he duly provided. His time sheets were works of art. He had a beautiful copperplate hand. His one failing, and it has been the failing of many a good man and woman, was the drink. Beside Gills was a store house that held barrels of ale belonging to the Bass Carrington Brewery. Now the odd time when Billy was tempted to go in for a quick one, he would invariably come out the worst for the wear. As far as I can recollect he was met with forbearance and tact from all concerned.

When I was sixteen I was offered an apprenticeship as a chaser. Bobby McGrath was the chaser in Gill's at this time. I jumped at the chance. My first job was chasing the tassels for the bottom of a sanctuary lamp. These sanctuary lamps were about 16" in dia. and had simple interlaced panels chased on them. When I started my apprenticeship Gills paid for my tuition at the College of art where I went at night. I was also allowed, nay encouraged, to make copies of pages from the *Book of Kells* and try to create original metalwork in the style of Irelands Golden Age. Bobby left Gills to join the Signals Corps of the British Army and David Hickey the chaser at Gills before McGrath came back from England to work for the firm again, for a short time.

I worked away and at night, when not attending the Art School, I made oil paintings from post cards for a man called Joe Brennan who provided me with the cards. Joe was one of the salesmen in Gills shop and he paid me a pound for each one. It was not chickenfeed. I also loved to visit the museums and galleries. At this time the National Museum of Ireland had plaster cast replicas of the High Crosses on display in the foyer with pictures of other heritage sites around the walls I used to cycle to some of sites that were near, such as Clondalkin where there is a Round Tower and Swords, where I live now. Back then it was exotic and far away from where I lived in Killester, relatively speaking. I visited Blackrock, where there are the remains of an ancient small cross with a face carved on it and St Douloughs Church and cross, the shape of which is echoed by the Penal Crosses which was also the inspiration for one of my earliest pieces of jewellery. I even cycled all the way to Glendalough in County Wicklow, where I spent the night in a youth hostel.

The other silversmithing and Ecclesiastical art metal working firms operating in Dublin at this time were Gunning's, that was by far the biggest producer of sacred metalwork and they exported all over the world. One of their most famous pieces is the stunning Fatima Monstrance. Smyths, of Wicklow Street, was another firm. You also had

The silversmiths shop at Alwright and Marshall. 1980. The chasers worked at the bench in the foreground. Photo by Gerry Brady, National Folklore Collection, University College Dublin

Matt Stanton on Dawson Street who made the iconic Sam Maguire Cup for Hopkins & Hopkins. And up the end of Harcourt Street was the Jewellery and Metal Company. This was not considered a real silversmithing firm by the men I worked with.

I left Gills to go to work in Alwright & Marshals Silversmiths in Fade Street when I was eighteen. Alwrights as we called it was a lot different from Gills in the fact that it concentrated on domestic silverware as opposed to Ecclesiastical ware. Even though the first thing I was shown when I went there were the patterns the firm made for their replica of the Cross of Cong. They did make the odd chalice as well. A feature of all these firms, the craftsmen took an interest and great pride in the work that was produced by their firm. Alwrights was also different from Gills in the way the work was fabricated, they had spinners. A spinner forced a metal disk over a chuck on a lathe to produce a form a whole lot quicker than one raised by hand

Alwrights started out as Wakley & Wheeler, an English firm. After Irish independence in 1922 they decided not to stay in the new state and in 1929 the owners left and sold the business to two of the workers, Johnny Alwright, a silversmith and freedom fighter as I was informed, and Jock Marshall a Scots Presbyterian and a chaser. An unlikely partnership but a very successful one. When I arrived Johnny had departed to his eternal reward. His wife Elizabeth, or Lizzie as she was known to all when she was not in earshot, was the boss and ran the place, ably assisted by Tony Marshall, the foreman silversmith and another great friend to me.

The building we worked in was a part of the South City Markets complex, it was three stories high. The spinners were on the ground floor, the polishing & plating on the next floor, Lizzie's office and the silver shop on the third floor. The silver shop was over an arcade and entrance to a meat factory, with a pillar holding up the entrance. This pillar would regularly get a belt by a lorry delivering product to the factory. Our workshop would rumble and shake, Working in the silver workshop was like working in a cathedral as from floor to ceiling it was about 24 feet high and one wall had Gothic style windows from wall to wall and from bench to ceiling.

Jock took me under his wing and gave me my head when I had not got a chasing job that was needed .When this happened he would tell me to cut up a piece of brass and chase a shield, usually with a Celtic or Shamrock design. I was given the freedom to decorate it as I saw fit. We had a pile of these shields a foot or so high of various shapes and sizes. When the workshop got the call for a sports trophy, one of the silversmiths rooted around in this pile until he found something that suited. It was the custom in Alwrights to take a plaster cast of all jobs we chased.

A lot of the articles produced in Alwrights were decorated with Celtic design. These included replicas of the Ardagh Chalice in many forms, including tea sets. The Dunvegan tea set was based on a medieval Maguire chalice that ended up in Dunvegan Castle on the Isle of Skye in Scotland. The Carroll tea set was also chased with interlacing. Salvers with interlaced borders were another popular item. As I browse the antique shops today I can see lots of silver plate that was

Alwright and Marshall at 14 Fade Street, Dublin as it appears in 2013.

made in Alwright & Marshalls. If you see something with the "Weirs" or "Wests" hallmark its odds-on it was made in Alwrights. Joe Dalton the polisher and plater related to me the story of how one of the young West's sons was apprenticed to Jock as a chaser. He was a bit of a playboy and tragically was killed driving a fast sports car. Weirs also had some kind of special relationship with Alwrights. Sydney Booth, Weirs' representative, was around so often he was like a member of the staff. Jimmy Martin and Tommy Sharkey were two other chasers I worked alongside in Alwrights. Jimmy, he was a theatre buff, would regularly recite Molly Bloom's soliloquy from *Ulysses*. Tommy was renowned for being able to write the Lord's Prayer with a pencil on the back of a postage stamp.

Tony Marshall once told me that in the old days the chasers worked on the ground floor and there was beer on draft in the workshop to make it attractive for the chasers to stay in the workshop.

Workbench at Alwright and Marshall 1980. Photo by Bróna Nic Amhlaoibh, , National Folklore Collection, University College Dublin.

Silver trophy made by Alwright and Marshall. Dublin hallmarks for 1963.

In 1965 the Second Vatican Council concluded. It was to usher in sweeping changes to the liturgy that changed the architecture of the churches as well as changing the rubrics regarding the composition of materials that could be used for scared vessels. Prior to Vatican II the cup of the chalice had to be made of silver and gilt inside. After the Vatican II a chalice could be made of ceramics or non-precious metal. By 1968 there were no silversmiths working in Gill's, Gunning's, Smyth's, or for that matter Stanton's. Gunnings had transformed itself into a company called Royal Irish Silver and they moved from Fleet

Silver Salver with Celtic border made at Royal Irish Silver, *Dublin hallmarks 1972*

Street, in what is now the fashionable Temple Bar area of Dublin, out to the Glasnevin Industrial Estate. I left Alwrights and went to work there in 1969. At one stage there were 120 employed there. There were six of us chasers and an apprentice working in our own wooden building. On a Monday morning it was the custom of the company to burst into song with,

> *"What will we do with the drunken chaser?*
> *What will we do with the drunken chaser?*
> *Put him in the pitch pot till he's sober*
> *Put him in the pitch pot till he's sober*
> *Ear-lie in the morning."*

The money was great in Royal Irish and the work was interesting. But I could not in all honesty say it was my favorite place to work. As far as I can remember we made very little Celtic style silver plate with the exception of Celtic salvers, it was mostly reproductions of Georgian silver. The Dairy Maid Tea service was the most popular and bestselling piece. All the people who worked in the silver trade at that time were members of The National Union of Gold, Silver & Allied Trades, an English trade union. Such were the contradictions in Ireland at that time. The trade was organized along clear lines of demarcation with a silversmith confining himself to what was considered a silversmith's work. For example, he would not polish or chase, and likewise a chaser would not polish or do silversmithing. It made some sense because a lot of the skills were very specialized.

However, when I left Royal Irish after two years I went to work in Irish Silver Ltd. situated off Meath Street, in an area known as the Liberties of Dublin. The workshop was an eighteenth century converted Quaker Meeting House building. The men agreed that I could move across the lines of demarcation because there was not enough chasing to keep a chaser employed for forty hours a week. I am very grateful to them for that. We made a fair number of Celtic style articles of silver plate and the signature Celtic piece would have been a rose bowl with pierced Celtic zoomorphic cover.

Irish Silver's proximity to St. Patrick's Cathedral gave me the opportunity to visit the cathedral on my lunch break. I loved looking at and studying the many memorials that adorned the walls, a number

Gold cross, Aidan Breen 1980.
Gift to his daughter Gráinne.

Letter "D" from the Book of Kells, silver brooch. Aidan Breen 1980s.

which were beautifully engraved brass plaques featuring Celtic interlacing.

While working in Irish Silver the work was short and we were put to a three day work week. I had started making Jewellery purely by accident. A friend had asked me to make him a Celtic cross and between one thing and another I started to get more requests for Jewellery. I had no formal training in Jewellery making, apart from my chasing and repoussé skills and the silversmithing skills I picked up in Irish Silver. I was well able to saw-pierce because as a child I used to do fretwork with the encouragement of my father, who was a joiner.

From the time I started working I have always done what we call "nixers", or working in my spare time for other companies. In Gills I had my paintings. When I worked in Alwrights, Paddy Malone, one of the silversmiths, introduced me to Lionel Mitchell, an antique dealer specializing in brass artifacts of every variety. I used to help him restore the decorated brass surrounds on Georgian fire places and the brass dials on grandfather clocks, as well as well as anything that was needed. Incidentally Lionel did not encourage me to make jewellery; he actually discouraged me, telling me "not to prostitute myself". He thought it would be better for me to concentrate on chasing. But when did I ever listen to anyone?

In 1978 this all resulted in me deciding to go out on my own and set up my own workshop doing what I knew best. Contract chasing and repoussé work for the trade and making jewellery using the Celtic design motifs I knew and loved. At this time I had been married to Mary for the last seven years and we had our two children Ciarán & Gráinne. My work was our only source of income. In 1979 I exhibited my work at the National Crafts Trade Fair, what is now known as "Showcase". The trade fair was held in the Royal Dublin Society exhibition hall in Ballsbridge, Dublin. When I started to show there, Pat Flood was the only other jeweler showing Celtic jewellery. Pat had a retail outlet in the Powerscourt Townhouse Shopping Centre in the city center.

I sold well at this fair. In Ireland in the nineteen eighties gold & silver Celtic Jewellery was considered high fashion and was bought by the great and the good. Over the years I got great orders at this fair for my Celtic jewellery, including a substantial one in the 1980s from Mervyn's, a department store in San Francisco. Later in the 1990s I had a terrific order from the Discovery Channel. I am delighted to report that it is

Five Bird Necklace, Aidan Breen*, based on the birds on the back of the hoop of the Tara Brooch.*

becoming very fashionable again. That said, I have always had a market for my Celtic jewellery.

I was also delighted to reestablish contact with Alwright & Marshals and to again do their chasing. And one of the jobs that gave me great pleasure was a Dish Ring (a particularly Irish form of silverware) I chased to celebrate Tony Marshal's fifty years of service with the firm.

George Bellew was another silversmithing firm I did chasing for. One of these jobs was what, a few of us referred to as, "Sons of Sam". These were miniature Sam Maguire Cups and I could not count the number made. I made Celtic design patterns for embellishing book covers and the Rivers of Ireland heads for spoon handles based on figure sculptures from Dublin's Custom House on the river Liffey.

Basil Clancy's Ogham Crafts was also another firm I worked for. I particularly remember the whiskey measures and bookmarks I chased with "Man Bites Dog" logo. This was a design showing an interlaced man biting a dog and decorated Donal Foleys humorous column that ran in the Irish Times from 1971 to 1981. This was sold through the Irish Times General Services, an adjunct to the Irish Times newspaper. At this time they also sold my jewellery and silver boxes. These boxes were inspired by the sculptured stones from the Irish country side that ranged from the Stone Age to the Early Medieval period.

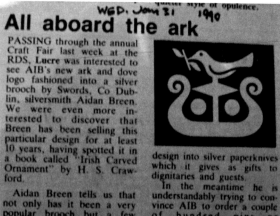

Irish Times, January 31, 1990.

Silver Brooch, Aidan Breen. *Zoomorphic design adapted from the reverse of the Tara Brooch.*

Jim Byrne was also a man I did chasing and pattern making for. One that sticks out was a chased portrait of P. H. Pearse, the leader of the 1916 Rising. I also chased strawberry dishes with scenes of Dublin for him. Jim once commissioned me to make an exact replica on a Corget as the Glenasheen Collar. Not in gold, but in copper that was gilded. He had his shop on Dawson Street back then. He is now in South Anne St.

One of my most popular pieces of jewellery was Noah's Ark, based on a design from a High Cross at Killary, Co. Meath. It featured a stylized boat, the ark with two faces peeping out and the dove of peace perched on top with the olive branch. I made it in brooches, pendants, and paperknives. The paperknives I sold to the Dept. of Foreign Affairs for use as gifts. I made a large one in copper for the Glencree Peace and Reconciliation Center as a wall hanging. The piece was very popular because of its association with peace, much sought in Ireland at that time because of turmoil created by the Provisional IRA's campaign of terror. This all changed when the now disgraced Allied Irish Bank paid a small fortune to a British company to design a new logo which, guess what?, came up with a variation of the design I had been using. I got in touch with them and explained my connection with the design, as a sop they ordered about a dozen paperknives. But as a piece of jewellery that was the end of that. AIB ruined the design for me, but about twenty eight years later, they, along with a number of other banks, ruined this proud country.

My good friends Des Taffe and Michael Hilliar are another two silversmiths I have worked for. Michael is the creator of the famous History of Ireland range of jewellery. I worked with Des when he came to Alwrights with another silversmith and two polishers via Staunton's, in a marriage arranged by Weir's. Des would have been well acquainted with the Dunvegan Tea set and amazingly Des was commissioned some years later by "the Maguire" (the Chief of the Maguire clan) to make an exact replica of the Dunvegan Cup. "The Maguire" considered this cup to be a Chalice associated with the Maguire family and Des Taffe delivered the finished Chalice to the National Museum of Ireland in the last few years. Michael and Des both worked together when Weir's reopened Matt Staunton's old workshop on Dawson Street in 1972 under the name of Dublin Silver.

The silversmiths James Mary Kelly and Dessie Byrne were two silversmiths I have had the pleasure of working with. I chased the Celtic knotwork on the two replicas of the Liam MacCarthy Cup for the G.A.A. This is the trophy presented to the winners of the All-Ireland Hurling Championship. It was a real treat to be involved in this work as the original was made by Edmond Johnson, of whose work I am a big fan. Ollie Ennis chased the first Sam Maguire for Des Byrne and I chased the most recent one. The Sam Maguire Cup is presented to the winners of the All-Ireland Gaelic Football Championship.

In 2005 the Dublin Assay Office commissioned me to follow my heart's desire and make a piece for their collection. I chose to make a two foot high silver sculpture based on James Joyce's masterpiece *Ulysses*. It's in the form of a Moorish tower set in a bed of blooms. The two smaller towers on top of the main tower are decorated by flat chasing with my idea of Moorish interlacing and the main tower has eighteen chased and repoussé panels representing the 18 episodes of Ulysses spiraling up the Tower. Each panel is decorated with my take on the episode. James Joyce was a great fan of the *Book of Kells* and it inspired him in the writing of *Ulysses*.

In conclusion looking back I have had a very hit-and-miss career and would certainly not consider myself a role model for anyone, except maybe how not to do it. But having said all that, I have had a very interesting and enjoyable time. My work has allowed me the privilege of meeting extremely talented and interesting people.

I have no intention of quitting the work I do and have ideas for making a few large pieces of silver. One of which is a vessel celebrating Joyce's *Finnegans Wake*, the other is *The Táin*, featuring the exploits of CúChulainn.   *AJB*

Ulysses Tower, Aidan Breen, 2009 Sterling silver, 22 x 11 inch height/base. Panels are 3 x 3.25 inches. Photos by Syd Bluett.

Early Waterhouse *mark from a Royal Tara Brooch.*

Later Waterhouse *mark on a University Brooch. The engraving, which was added when the brooch was given as a gift, dates this piece to 1904.*

Hallmarks from the Dunvegan Teapot pictured on page 14. The crowned "W" is West's *registered assay mark, the seated Hibernia figure represents the Dublin Assay Office, The crowned harp indicates sterling silver and the letter "T" for the year 1914.*

Maker's Marks and Hallmarks

Although the marking and selling of precious metals is highly regulated by law in the United Kingdom and Ireland, much of the Celtic jewellery that is encountered from the 19th and 20th centuries is not marked according to the conventional standard.

Legally, any object that is silver or gold over a minimum weight is supposed to be submitted to a government chartered Assay Office for random testing for metal quality and hallmarking. The maker can apply the maker's mark, also called the "sponsor's mark". Three other marks are applied at the Assay Office which indicate the quality of the metal, such as sterling silver or the different carats of gold, a letter mark for the year it was assayed and a stamp for the office that verifies the claim of precious metal content. This system is of great value to collectors as it tells with certainty who, what, where and when a piece was made.

While the hallmark system ensures a degree of consumer protection and gives the producer a solid claim to legitimate trading, submitting work for assay entails time and expense. From 1784 to 1890 an additional mark, the sovereign's head, called the "duty mark" indicated that the piece had been taxed.

Few of the Irish Celtic Revival pieces are hallmarked, although many are stamped with a maker's mark. In the case of Waterhouse & Co., some clue as to date can be gained because the mark changed with time. Earlier Royal Tara Brooches were manufactured by stamping in dies and the maker's mark, "WATERHOUSE & Co." and a separate mark "DUBLIN" were impressed on the backs of the brooches with recessed letters. Later Royal Tara Brooches were manufactured by casting. These had raised letters in a recessed rectangle. Other makers sometimes put their makers mark in the mould or pattern that produced the pieces. The Cavan Brooch was produced with the words " WEST & Sons, Dublin, Registered 1849" right in the tooling. In this manner brooches made decades later would still bear the date 1849.

Scottish agate jewellery is also usually made with no marks at all, however occasionally pieces turn up with lozenge marks, which were used as a system of patent registration. This system was in use in Great Britain from 1842 to 1883. The Celebrated Iona Cross brooch on page 36 bears the lozenge registration mark for December 1883.

The earliest Iona jewellery attributable to Alexander and Euphemia Ritchie was hallmarked by the London firm of Cornelius Saunders and Francis Shepard, who manufactured in Birmingham and Chester. Their mark "CS*FS" can be seen on both of the Galley Sheild brooches on pages 40 & 41. Many Ritchie pieces turn up without assay marks. He could easily avoid since he was working , largely to a tourist market, far from the centers of authority during a time when the practice of submitting silver jewellery for assay was just beginning to be commonly practiced. When Iain McCormick began producing silver jewellery on his own he was haphazard about submitting it for assay and often marked the pieces "STERLING" and "SCOTLAND" as well as the "IONA" mark. This method of marking would be very familiar to Canadian and American where it is common for jewelers to mark 925 silver with the word "STERLING" rather than using the symbols of the assay system.

Fully hallmarked Alexander Ritchie *penannular brooch. Two versions of the "A.R." stamp, "IONA", a patent registration & Glasgow hallmarks for 1928-29.*

The mark of the person or company submitting work for assay is technically called the "sponsor's mark" as there is no requirement that the piece be submitted by the actual maker, however, it is commonly called the "maker's mark". Craftsmen use it as a signature as well. Many brass pieces made by Ritchie and other's are stamped with their registered sponsor's mark as a way of branding the work. There is no requirement that brass, copper or other base metals be marked, but pride of workmanship and the added value of a well respected craftsman signing the work makes it a common practice.

The reverse of a detail of the MacLean's Cross brooch shown on page ___. Marked "IMC" for Iain McCormick, "STERLING" and "SCOTLAND". This piece is not properly hallmarked but could be excused if the piece was sold for export.

A sponsor's mark is a set of initials that is registered with the assay office. Since more than one person or company may have the same initials, the shape of the punch must also be unique in combination with the letters. Craftsmen with long careers often register different marks as time goes on. The photo at the top of this page shows two variations on Alexander Ritchie's "AR" mark, but he also is known to have registered "AER" for Alexander and Euphemia Ritchie and "ICA" for Iona Celtic Art.

Reverse of a GAA football medal. "J.M.Co." is the Jewelry Metal Co. *Dublin marks for 1958*

To the collector, an unmarked or un-assayed piece can be admired for the rebel spirit of the maker, who dodged the taxes and refused the burdens of time and cost. But on the other hand the assay marks tell a very reliable story about when and where a piece was made, which is of great interest, as well as an assurance of quality , age and origin.

SAW

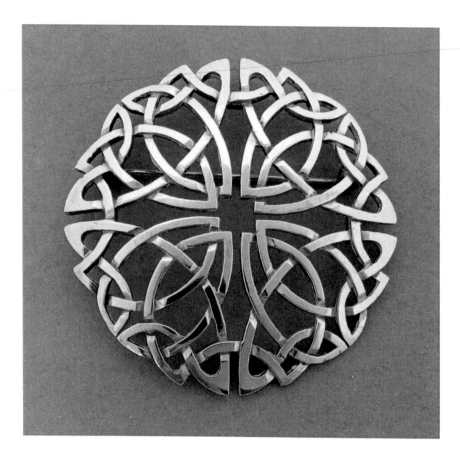

Continuum

Several beliefs that have emerged since the 19th century have become popular, non-academic folk-interpretations of Celtic art. The nearly miraculous technical complexity and imagination exhibited in the original masterpieces, such as the *Book of Kells* or the *Tara Brooch*, have been described as "The Work of Angels". The qualities of these accomplishments are the product of gifted hands and minds, imagined to border on the supernatural. A sense of awe about the original medieval work is a big part of the message of modern Celtic art.

It is also a cultural theme that the style is purely native. A very chauvinistic exaggeration was stated by Henry O'Neill in his book *Illustrations of the Round Towers of Ireland* (Dublin 1877), *"In the fine arts the Ancient Irish were not influenced by the styles of other nations which had attained to great artistic excellence; the Irish invented a national style of art quite distinct from every other country, and in it they displayed a power of composition, colouring, and above all, of miraculous executive ability never equaled by any other people."* The style is thus useful as a proud, even boastful emblem of national identity in its modern expression. In truth the art absorbed many foreign influences and was in fact an international style in early medieval northwestern Europe.

There is a prevailing folklore that each element, each knot, spiral or interlaced animal, is a symbol. The notion that there is some sort of secret language to Celtic ornament is widespread and persistent. One of the most common questions from the general public about Celtic jewellery is, "what does it mean?" The creators and purveyors of modern Celtic jewellery, and other articles decorated with Celtic ornament, sometimes offer very responsible educational explanations for their wares, but others have taken a great deal of liberty.

There is a stubborn expectation that any meaning for this ancient style should be the same today as it was fourteen hundred years ago. What meaning, if any, the ornamental details held in medieval times are sometimes unknowable. Certain motifs have well established symbolic meaning. Crosses, christograms, symbols of the Four Evangelists (Matthew, Mark, Luke and John), and other widely used Christian religious signs are relatively obvious. The animals of Celtic interlace are often difficult to identify by species, but the zoomorphics of the original artifacts many can be read as hounds, peacocks, doves or eagles, all of which have well established traditional symbolic meaning. Other species have been added in the modern revival. Spirals and knots are less certain as anything other than ornament. But this does not stop them from being supplied with meaning as they come to be used very differently by modern designers and artists. The most widely used knotwork symbolism is the "Trinity knot" or triquetra. This simple and beautiful knot has been consciously used as a Christian symbol during the 150 years of the Celtic Revival. In recent decades Pagan revivalists have also appropriated it as an emblem of the "Triple Goddess". This concept, stripped of its religious overtones, is now frequently presented as an appropriate gift for a grandmother to give her daughter and granddaughter as a token of the *three ages of woman*.

The *Tara Brooch* was certainly a symbol of high status for its original owner in the 8th century. It is unlikely that the medieval designer intended anything like the symbol of national identity that it became after Waterhouse's promotion of it in the 19th century. The style of the *Book of Kells* was an international style when it was made for the Glory of God, but the revival of that style was practiced for the glory of the race and nation.

A standard. answer to the 'meaning of knotwork' question in recent times is that Celtic knots are endless paths and so represent eternity or continuum. The Scottish art teacher George Bain published the book *Celtic Art; The Methods of Construction* in 1951. This book became a standard reference and source book, especially after its re-release in 1973. In it the author made a great deal of the *single continuous path* that is laid out in many ancient knotwork panels. This observation leads quite nicely to ideas about the "circle of life" or "never ending… love, faith, loyalty". These can be seen as metaphors for the interwoven-ness of life, or linking knots are frequently referred to as "love knots." To some these seem like trite, pat answers to the question of meaning, which may have more to do with marketing than with any authentic tradition. But marketing is also part of the culture.

Why would it be that *continuum* would be such an important concept that an elaborate symbology as knotwork would be contrived? In modern times those who maintain an interest in Celtic things relate to the idea of continuum in their desire to affirm and preserve a culture they value, nobly surviving despite centuries on the margins of European mainstream. Celtic Diaspora, whose interest in their roots have become a passion, especially relate to a message of continuum, as they strive to identify with their heritage in the multi-cultural melting pot. If the modern motive for creating or viewing Celtic art involves a sense of heritage, the message of continuum works.

The folklore of Celtic art flows together for the modern Celt through the experience of multiple revivals, each of which reached for its own connection to the past. The beauty of the designs and the nostalgia for an idealized heritage that they evoke makes the style of art itself a mysterious emblem of identity and pride. *SAW*

Glossary

Agate – a type of igneous stone that because it is hard, tight grained and brightly coloured is frequently used in jewellery. Agates were so commonly used in Victorian Scottish pebble jewellery that the type is often referred to as "Scottish agate" even when other stones are used.

Cabochon – a gem stone or glass stud which is shaped and polished with a convex dome or flat top. A "carbuncle" is a domed cabochon garnet.

Assay – the process of testing precious metals for quality. In many European countries, including Ireland and the United Kingdom, precious metals must be submitted for assay before they are hallmarked.

Carat - A quality designation for gold. 24 carat gold is pure, 18 carat is 18/24 or 75% pure. Abbreviated "Ct." In the United States it is spelled "karat" and abbreviated "K. Carat is also a unit of weight for precious stones.

Casting - A method of shaping metal by pouring liquid molten metal into a mould. The objects in this book are cast into either sand moulds or by lost-wax casting. Sand casting creates a mould from sand that uses clay and/or oil as a binder. An impression is made in the sand using a model, which is then copied in metal when the impression is filled with liquid metal. Lost wax casting creates a void in a clay or plaster based mould by encapsulating a wax model, which is removed by heating the mould until the wax melts and burns away. The lost-wax process is also called *cire-perdu* or investment moulding.

Chasing - the method of tooling metal with blunt chisels, often while the piece is supported in pitch.

Electrotype – a method of filling a mould with metal by running current through a liquid solution containing metal that is deposited on the surface of a mould in the manner of electroplating, but much thicker.

Engraving- letters, shapes or designs are carved or scratched into the surface of metal with a sharp chisel-like tool.

Gilt or Gilding - Covering an object with a thin layer of gold. This can be done in several ways, such as electrically plating using gold dissolved from a liquid solution, applying very thin sheets of gold leaf or by painting the piece with a liquid solution of gold dissolved in mercury, which is heated to drive off the mercury as a vapor.

Hallmark – a punch or impression used to mark precious metals that certify who made the object, what it is made of, when it was tested and where the testing was carried out. In Ireland and the United Kingdom hallmarks are carried out at a government chartered Assay Office.

Penannular brooch – a variation on a ring brooch where a pin is held in place by a C-shaped brooch with enlarged terminals. The pin is linked to the hoop of the C so that it can after the pin has passed into and out of the fabric. The end of the pin passes forward through the gap between the terminals and the body of the brooch twists to a locking position where the end of the pin rests in front of the brooch.

Pictish – Refers to the early medieval culture of the Picts in North-East Scotland.

Pseudo-penannular brooch – A brooch type that shares the attractive shape of a penannular brooch but lacks the gap. The Tara and Hunterston brooches are both pseudo-penannular.

Repoussé – an ornamental technique by which metal is hammered or punched from the back to create relief patterns. Often used in tandem with chasing from the front.

Stamping – dies, usually carved from steel, are used to press designs into and cut shapes in metal.

Sterling Silver- a quality standard of purity that is 925/1000 pure silver, usually alloyed with copper.

Bibliography

Bain, George. *Celtic Art; The Methods of Construction*. New York: Dover Publications, Inc., 1973.

Bodkin, Thomas. "The Arts and Crafts Society of Ireland." *The Studio Magazine*. 15 December 1921: Page 257-266.

Dawes, Ginny Reddington, Corrinne Davidov, and Tom Dawes. *Victorian Jewellery. Unexplored Treasures*, New York: Abbeville Press, 1991.

Drummond, James. *Sculptured Monuments in Iona & the West Highlands*. Edinburgh: Society of Antiquaries of Scotland, 1881.

Edelstein, Terri J., and Michael Camille. *Imagining an Irish past; The Celtic Revival, 1840-1940*. Chicago: David and Alfred Smart Museum of Art,1992.

Finlay, Ian. *Scottish Crafts*. London: G.G. Harrap, 1948.

Graham, Henry Davenport. *Antiquities of Iona*. London: Day & Son, 1850.

Joyce, Cecily. *Claddagh Ring Story*. Galway: Clodoiri Lurgan Teo, 1991.

Karkov, Catherine E., Robert T. Farrell, and Michael Ryan. *The Insular Tradition*. Albany: State University of New York Press, 1997.

Larmour, Paul. *The Arts and Crafts Movement in Ireland*. Belfast: Friar's Bush Press, 1992.

MacArthur, E. Mairi. *Iona Celtic Art; The Work of Alexander and Euphemia Ritchie*. Isle of Iona: New Iona Press, 2003.

MacCormick, Iain and Alexander Ritchie. *The Celtic Art of Iona: Drawings and Reproductions from the Manuscripts of the Late Alex Ritchie of Iona, and from the Iona Press of 1887* . Isle of Iona: New Iona Press, 1994.

O'Neill, Henry. *Illustrations of the Most Interesting Sculptured Crosses in Ancient Ireland*, London: H. O'Neill,1857.

O'Neill, Henry. *The Round Towers of Ireland*. Dublin: M. H. Gill & Son, 1887.

Pickford, Ian. *Jackson's Hallmarks*, Woodbridge: Antique Collectors Club Ltd, 1991.

Scarisbrick, Diana. *Scottish Jewellery: a Victorian Passion*. Milan: Harry N. Abrams, 2009.

Shaw-Smith, David. *Traditional Crafts of Ireland*, New York: Thames and Hudson, 1984.

Sheehy, Jeanne. *The Rediscovery of Ireland's Past; The Celtic Revival 1830-1930*. London: Thames and Hudson, 1980.

Stokes, Margaret MacNair. *Early Christian Art in Ireland*. Dublin: Champman and Hall Ltd., 1927.

Young, Susan, Paul T. Craddock, and National Museums of Scotland. *The Work of Angels; Masterpieces of Celtic Metalwork, 6th -9th centuries AD*. Austin: University of Texas Press, 1990.

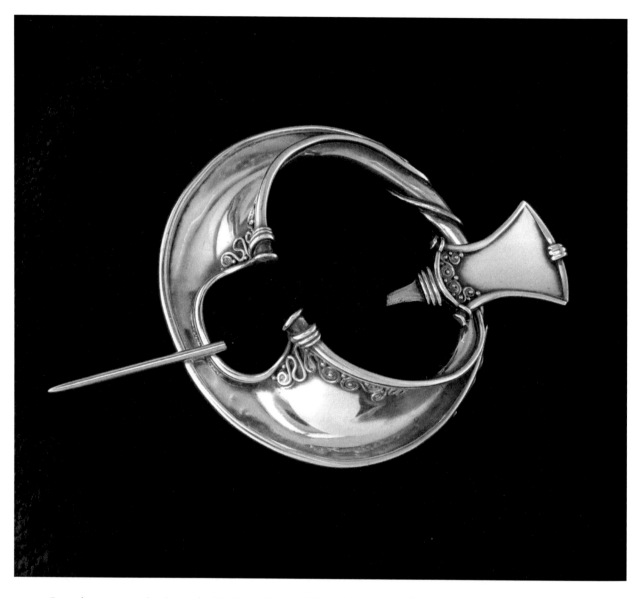

Pseudo-penannular brooch. Sterling silver & 18K gold 2.5 inch diameter. Stephen Walker 1980.

36017565R00042

Made in the USA
San Bernardino, CA
16 May 2019